This item was purchased through funds
provided by the Consortium of Academic
and Research Libraries in Illinois (CARLI).

The
Navajo People
and
Uranium Mining

D1596574

THE
Navajo People
AND
Uranium Mining

EDITED BY

Doug Brugge
Timothy Benally
AND Esther Yazzie-Lewis

FOREWORD BY Stewart L. Udall

UNIVERSITY OF NEW MEXICO PRESS
ALBUQUERQUE

© 2006 by the University of New Mexico Press
All rights reserved. Published 2006
Printed in the United States of America

First paperbound printing, 2007
Paperbound ISBN: 978-0-8263-3779-5

12 11 10 09 08 07   1 2 3 4 5 6

Library of Congress Cataloging-in-Publication Data

Brugge, Doug.
  The Navajo people and uranium mining / Doug Brugge,
Timothy Benally, Esther Yazzie-Lewis.
      p. cm.
  Includes bibliographical references and index.
  ISBN-13: 978-0-8263-3778-8 (cloth : alk. paper)
  ISBN-10: 0-8263-3778-3 (cloth : alk. paper)
  1. Navajo Indians—Interviews. 2. Navajo Indians—Diseases.
  3. Navajo Indians—Health and hygiene. 4. Uranium mines
and mining—Health aspects—Southwestern States.
  5. Uranium miners—Diseases—Southwestern States.
  I. Benally, Timothy. II. Yazzie-Lewis, Esther, 1950– III. Title.
  E99.N3B785 2006
  363.17'99—dc22
                                   2006026325

**Cover photograph by Milton Snow,
courtesy of the Navajo Nation Museum,
Window Rock, AZ, Catalog #NG6–52.**

Book design and composition by Damien Shay
Body type is Utopia 10.5/14
Display is Radiant and Trade Gothic

To my father, DAVID BRUGGE,
my wife, PHYLLIS FONSECA,
our daughter CAMILLE,
and to the Navajo people
with whom I grew up.
— DB

To my wife, KAREN BENALLY,
my children and grandchildren,
and to the people in the communities
who contributed to the book.
— TB

To my late father and mother,
PETER and MARY DENNISON,
and family who supported my efforts
for social justice throughout the years,
and to the Navajo people who have
fallen victim of uranium exploitation.
— EY-L

Royalties from the sale
of this book will support the
Navajo Uranium Memorial.

Contents

LIST OF ILLUSTRATIONS   x

FOREWORD *Stewart L. Udall*   xi

ACKNOWLEDGMENTS   xiii

INTRODUCTION   xv
"So a lot of the Navajo ladies became widows"
> *Doug Brugge, Timothy Benally, and Esther Yazzie-Lewis*

CHAPTER ONE   1
Leetso, the Powerful Yellow Monster:
A Navajo Cultural Interpretation of Uranium Mining
> *Esther Yazzie-Lewis and Jim Zion*

CHAPTER TWO   11
"I have revisited the places where I used to work":
Oral History of Former Miner George Tutt
> *Interview in Navajo by Timothy Benally, December 1995*
> *Translation/transcription by Esther Yazzie-Lewis and Timothy Benally*

CHAPTER THREE   25
A Documentary History of Uranium Mining
and the Navajo People
> *Doug Brugge and Rob Goble*

CHAPTER FOUR 49
"Human beings are priceless":
Interview with Leroy and Lorraine Jack
Interview in Navajo by Phil Harrison, December 1995
Translation/transcription by Esther Yazzie-Lewis and Timothy Benally

CHAPTER FIVE 57
Advocacy and Social Action among Navajo People:
Uranium Workers and their Families, 1988–1995
Susan E. Dawson, Perry H. Charley, and Phillip Harrison Jr.

CHAPTER SIX 79
"Our children are affected by it":
Oral History of Former Miner George Lapahie
Interview in Navajo by Timothy Benally, December 1995
Translation/transcription by Esther Yazzie-Lewis and Timothy Benally

CHAPTER SEVEN 89
Psychological Effects of Technological/
Human-Caused Environmental Disasters:
Examination of the Navajo People and Uranium
Carol A. Markstrom and Perry H. Charley

CHAPTER EIGHT 117
"It was like slave work":
Oral History of Miner Tommy James
Interview in Navajo by Phil Harrison, December 1995
Translation/transcription by Esther Yazzie-Lewis and Timothy Benally

CHAPTER NINE 129
"Everything has been ruined for us":
Oral History of Miner Joe Ray Harvey
Interview in Navajo by Phil Harrison, December 1995
Translation/transcription by Esther Yazzie-Lewis and Timothy Benally

CHAPTER TEN   137
The Radiation Exposure Compensation Act:
What Is Fair?

Doug Brugge and Rob Goble

CHAPTER ELEVEN   155
"We will never forget it":
Oral History of Widows Mary Louise Johnson
and Minnie Tsosie

Interview in Navajo by Timothy Benally, December, 1995
Translation/transcription by Esther Yazzie-Lewis and Timothy Benally

CHAPTER TWELVE   167
Eastern Navajo Diné Against Uranium Mining:
Interview with Rita and Mitchell Capitan

From the film Homeland: Four Portraits of Native Action, *2005,*
Katahdin Foundation / Update by Chris Shuey

APPENDIX   177
The Navajo Uranium Miner Oral History
and Photography Project

Doug Brugge and Timothy Benally

INDEX   199

List of Illustrations

Fig. 2.1   George Tutt Sr., Oak Springs, 1995.   12

Fig. 2.2   Miner riding small rail car.   18

Fig. 3.1   Map of the Navajo Nation with uranium   28
            areas marked on it.

Fig. 3.2   Navajo miners dumping low-grade ore.   29

Fig. 4.1   Leroy and Lorraine Jack, Cudei, NM, 1995.   50

Fig. 5.1   Phil Harrison, Mitten Rock, AZ, 1995.   61

Fig. 6.1   George Lapahie, Two Grey Hills, 1995.   80

Fig. 7.1   Mary Frank, Red Valley/Oak Springs/   90
            Shiprock, 1995.

Fig. 7.2   Helen Johnson, Shiprock, NM, 1995.   98

Fig. 8.1   Tommy James, Cove, AZ, 1995.   118

Fig. 9.1   Joe Ray Harvey, Cove, AZ, 1995.   130

Fig. 11.1   Mary Louise Johnson, Mitten Rock, NM, 1995.   156

Fig. 11.2   Minnie Tsosie, Cove, AZ, 1995.   157

Fig. 12.1   Rita and Mitchell Capitan with son.   168

Foreword

To fully understand the tragic experience of the Navajo People with uranium mining, you have to consider how the Navajos lived a half-century ago. As a result of humanitarian failures of the national government, that generation of Navajos did not have access to rudimentary education. They had not held industrial jobs previously, and had no knowledge of the existence of radiation or of the dangers that it held for them in the underground mines where they worked. Mining was an important source of income for many Navajos, so they went to work for mining companies producing ore for the U.S. government. It was only after an epidemic of lung cancer and other respiratory illnesses appeared years later that miners were told the truth by their government.

Where native people are illiterate, the U.S. government has a special trust relationship that involves both legal and moral responsibilities. Such a duty was never discharged with respect to the Navajo uranium miners. Despite the entreaties of U.S. Public Health officials who carried out a study of the health of uranium miners, the Atomic Energy Commission simply walked away and left the situation in the hands of the mining companies and the states, who knew little about the hazards. The result was a tragedy, as innocent people were exposed to high levels of lethal radiation.

I first became involved with the Navajo People's tragic experience with uranium mining in 1978. At that time, I was hopeful that compensation for the uranium miners could be achieved through litigation aimed at the federal government. That effort failed due to the "sovereign immunity" doctrine shield evoked by the government. As I have written previously,[1] I was devastated by the federal court's decision and deeply troubled by the failure to achieve justice. In the end, legislation was finally passed by the U.S. Congress and was signed into law in 1990.

But the story did not end there. The original compensation program was flawed, and was amended ten years later under pressure from the affected communities and federal health officials. Looking back, it is striking how many decades passed from the first mining in the late 1940s to the present, and how slow compensation was in coming. I worked on the claim cases of Navajo miners and their widows in the 1990s.

It is overdue for this volume to appear. After all these years of hardship, ending in a bare semblance of justice, there are important moral lessons to be learned. The oral histories and narrative chapters in this volume may help public-health officials and people in high places to gain some empathy for the poor and the disadvantaged. Oral history, in particular, can be very moving. I hope that these stories and these statements will be widely read, and that in some small way they will contribute to the prevention of future avoidable tragedies of this kind. The Navajo uranium miners and their families were literally sacrificed to help the nation prevail in the Cold War.

Stewart L. Udall

2006

Notes

1.   See S. L. Udall, *The myths of August: A personal exploration of our tragic cold war affair with the atom* (New York: Pantheon Books, 1994).

Acknowledgments

First and foremost, we want to thank the miners, widows, and children who consented to be interviewed. Their willingness to share their experiences, pain, and suffering, along with their incredible courage and perseverance, are a testament to the strength and endurance of the Navajo people. We thank the following Navajo people who were interviewed as part of an oral-history project that one of us directed, and who taught us so much about their experience and the issue of uranium mining in their communities: Logan Pete, Floyd Frank, Leroy and Virginia Deal, Donald Yellowhorse, Boyde Tsosie, Thomas Woolboy, George Tutt, Thomas Benally, George Lapahie, Taylor Dixon, Julia Yazzie, Dan N. Benally, Paul Nakaidenae, Anna Aloysious, Tom James, Edison Tyler, Mae John, Helen Johnson, Joe Ray Harvey, Kathlene Tsosie, Dorothy Zohnnie, Leroy and Lorraine Jack, Mary Frank, Mary Louise Johnson, Minnie Tsosie, and Pearl Nakai.

We also thank the authors who contributed narrative chapters to this volume. Their intellectual work has often been carried out in relative obscurity and with little or no funding, but always in the hope that their efforts will help prevent future disasters such as this one, and that they might possibly help bring some justice to the Navajo uranium communities. We thank the Navajo Nation Museum for preserving the photographs and providing them for reproduction. We also thank Phyllis Fonseca and an anonymous reviewer for reading and commenting on the manuscript, and Bindu Panikkar for assisting with its preparation. The editors thank Barbara Fitch Cobb for her thorough copy editing.

Chapter Three

We thank Ken Silver and David Brugge for commenting on the manuscript, and Janelle Bagley and Sabine Jean-Louie for assistance with preparing it.

Chapter Five

The authors would like to thank Gary Madsen for reviewing this chapter.

Chapter Ten

The authors thank Timothy Benally, Perry Charley, Helen Johnson, Esther Yazzie-Lewis, Christine Benally, and Phillip Harrison for teaching them the things about RECA that cannot be learned from a book.

Appendix

The Navajo Uranium Miner Oral History and Photography Project was supported by funding from the U.S. EPA, the Educational Foundation, the Ruth Mott Fund, the Ford Foundation, and hundreds of generous individual donations.

This book was reviewed and approved by the
Navajo Nation Human Research Review Board.

"SO A LOT OF THE NAVAJO LADIES BECAME WIDOWS"

Doug Brugge, Timothy Benally,
and Esther Yazzie-Lewis
September 2005

The Navajo Nation covers a vast stretch of northeastern
Arizona and parts of New Mexico and Utah in the southwestern United States. It is home to the majority of the more
than 250,000 members of the Navajo Tribe who live in sparsely
populated small towns and isolated homesteads that dot the
countryside. The Navajo lands range from desolate stretches of
rock and dirt, to lush mountains, to strikingly beautiful sandstone canyons, to volcanic stone monuments that rise precipitously above the plains.

It is also home to more than 1,000 abandoned uranium
mines and four former uranium mills, a legacy of the U.S.
nuclear program that has left scars on the land and the people
to this day. And it is the Navajo people's experience with uranium, their unresolved grievances and the need to heal old
wounds, that prompted a team of Navajo people and supportive whites to undertake the Navajo Uranium Miner Oral
History and Photography Project from which this book arose.
The project team formed following discussions between two
of the editors (Brugge and Benally), one white and the other
Navajo. These two, once they decided that the project would be

a good one to pursue, recruited the rest of the project team into a collaboration that was majority Navajo, but based at Tufts University School of Medicine in Boston.

Historical Perspective

We set the context for the book by giving a brief overview of the history of the Navajo people with uranium based on an oral recording made by one of us (Benally). In the early 1940s, the Navajo Nation was still in the early stages of economic development, recovering from the devastating stock reduction period of the 1930s. To meet the economic gap that was created by this stock reduction, Navajo men sought work away from the reservation on railroads. Families who had no livestock sought farm work in Phoenix and California.

Employment sources at that time were the Bureau of Indian Affairs (BIA), traders on the reservation, and a few of the border-town businesses. Employment was based on the amount of education the person had—especially with the BIA, whose work force was about 90 percent Anglo. The Treaty of 1868 had given the federal government responsibility for Navajo education and health services. However, the Navajo people's needs became greater as the population increased.

When World War II broke out, many Navajo men aborted their education and went into the military. The few high schools in the Navajo Reservation were closed for lack of students. The Cold War followed the end of World War II, and the Navajo Nation was still dependent on the BIA for its economic needs. The Tribe now had a council and hired some of its own people. States and counties were getting involved in Navajo affairs.

As the United States entered the nuclear age, the Navajo Nation was still struggling economically. The U.S. government's demand for uranium initiated mining booms in the Four Corners area. Uranium was discovered in Cove, Arizona, and then in other parts of the reservation. Work became available right near home, and young Navajo men grabbed the jobs in the uranium mines. This was a time when transportation was still by horse-drawn wagons, horseback riding, and walking. In most communities, there were few motor vehicles.

When the mines started on the reservation, most families were very thankful that they had employment. Benally notes that when he was director of the Navajo Nation's Office of the Navajo Uranium Workers (ONUW), miners' wives and widows had a common refrain. They would say that they "were glad that our husbands had jobs and that they didn't have to go away to other places to do railroad work. The jobs were right here and they could go from home to the mine and it was great. But what the people that operated these mines didn't tell the Navajo people was the danger that was associated with uranium mining. If they had told us about the danger we might have done something else to find employment. But they didn't tell us and we just enjoyed our people working."

The federal government and the mining companies knew of the hazards of uranium mining, and the Public Health Service even conducted a study to document the development of illnesses that they expected. The miners and the widows, however, were never informed, and had to find out about the danger on their own, from witnessing and experiencing the sicknesses that developed in the wake of working in the mines. The stories that they tell are very sad. They say that they tried every kind of medicine. When they tried Western medicine, the doctors didn't know what was wrong with their husbands until they were diagnosed with lung cancer. Then they were told simply that they were dying.

So a lot of the Navajo ladies became widows. They acquired the responsibility that the miner had had at home, including a lot of the daily chores around the house, such as hauling and chopping the wood, hauling water, and feeding livestock. For the widows and children, the loss of their husbands and fathers created great hardships.

In 1960, the widows started coming together to talk about their husbands' deaths and how they had died. The gatherings occurred in the Red Rock Chapter near Shiprock, New Mexico. The meetings had a snowball effect, and more people came together—more widows, and sometimes children. They formed a committee, and the committee talked more and more about the death of the uranium miners.

The communities eventually hired an attorney to assist them, and after many years of struggle they got the Radiation Exposure Compensation Act (RECA) passed in 1990, which was supposed to provide "compassionate compensation" to miners and their survivors. Unfortunately, RECA fell short of being just compensation for many former miners and their families since they continued to have their claims denied. In 2000, RECA was amended to attempt to correct some of its shortcomings.

The Book

This book had a relatively long gestation period. In fact, the original steps along the path that eventually led to its publication were not directed toward this end. Rather, this book grew out of the Navajo Uranium Miner Oral History and Photography Project, which did its primary data collection in December of 1995. The objective of the work at that time was to produce a self-published booklet of considerably smaller scale than this one. The project did produce its booklet, and a video and exhibit as well. Those products, as successful as they were (see Appendix), utilized only excerpts from the oral histories and did not address the documentary history of the Navajo people with uranium mining.

This volume reproduces a subset of the oral histories in more complete form, and combines them with narrative chapters that assess the experience of the Navajo people with uranium from diverse perspectives (history, psychology, culture, advocacy, and policy). We do not try to present the experience wrapped up in a tidy package with a single internally consistent conclusion. While the points of view taken in different chapters are similar, there is considerable range of perspective. For example, all of the contributors to this volume would agree that the experience of the Navajo people with uranium was a tragedy and a violation of human rights; there are, however, a variety of conceptions of what would constitute justice.

In addition, chapters have distinctly different "voices." For example, chapter one is political and cultural in tone, chapter two is a verbatim transcript from an interview with a former miner, while chapter three is a scholarly rendition of history. We hope the range of perspectives and voices gives readers a deeper appreciation for the complexity of the issue and helps them understand that they do not know everything, even after finishing the book. Because of the range of voices and perspectives, we have allowed some information to be repeated in different ways in different chapters, sometimes with minor differences, reflecting varying understandings of underlying facts and events. It is possible to read many of the chapters out of order, or to read select chapters without reading the entire book.

We hope that the variety and range of analyses and voices prompt the reader to think more deeply about the issues involved, rather than coming to easier and neater conclusions.

Chapter One

LEETSO, THE POWERFUL YELLOW MONSTER

A NAVAJO CULTURAL INTERPRETATION OF URANIUM MINING

Esther Yazzie-Lewis and Jim Zion

The Name of the Monster

The Navajo Nation in Arizona, New Mexico, and Utah is the world's largest Indian nation. With more than 16 million acres of land, it is larger than Ireland and about one-fifth the size of Japan. It has the largest American Indian population in the United States, with over 255,000 enrolled members, 168,000 of whom live in the Navajo Nation. The Four Corners region of the American Southwest—named for the place where the states of Arizona, Utah, Colorado, and New Mexico come together—is where the largest quantities of uranium were mined in the United States. It is also the U.S. region with the highest American Indian population. Over 400,000 American Indians live in those four states. That is 20 percent of the total American Indian population.

The Navajo Nation is a nation, a nationality. As such, what do the Navajo people—*Diné* in the Navajo language—think about atomic energy? What do they think about modern uranium culture? How do Navajo people view the events of the

1

second half of the twentieth century, when military, political, and industrial factions used the power of radioactive materials to build political and economic power?

Navajo people do have points of view on these issues. They see uranium and materials for atomic power as a monster. The Navajo word for monster is *nayee.* The literal translation is "that which gets in the way of a successful life." Navajo people also believe that one of the best ways to start to overcome or weaken a monster as a barrier to life is to name it. Every evil—each monster—has a name. Uranium has a name in Navajo. It is *leetso,* which means "yellow brown" or "yellow dirt." Aside from its literal translation, the word carries a powerful connotation. Sometimes when we translate a Navajo word into English, we say it "sounds like" something. We think *leetso* sounds like a reptile, like a monster. It is a monster, as we will explain.

The Birth of *Leetso*

The monster was fertilized in 1896, when radioactivity was discovered, and again in 1898, when the Curies uncovered atomic energy. It took shape in 1934, when Enrico Fermi achieved nuclear fission, and on December 2, 1942, when the first successful nuclear chain reaction took place under a sports stadium at the University of Chicago. The monster was born on July 16, 1945, at Alamogordo, New Mexico, when the first atomic bomb was exploded.

The Navajo people were the midwife of the monster, although they did not know it at that time. The Bureau of Indian Affairs discovered a uranium/vanadium-bearing mineral in the Navajo Nation in 1941 (see chapter 3). At the same time, the Navajo Tribal Council passed a resolution to support the United States in opposition to the threat of Nazi Germany. By the time the war broke out in late 1941, Navajo people joined the war effort. Many enlisted in the American armed forces. They joined the military at rates far higher than the general population. Navajo patriots did not realize that they were a central part of the Manhattan Project, the military-civilian organization that built the first atomic bomb. Traditional Navajos would have been horrified had they known what others would do with their yellow dirt.

Navajo people also joined the Cold War. They again enlisted in the military to serve in Korea, Vietnam, and other places of confrontation. They also did their part on the nuclear front: Navajo lands contributed 13 million tons of uranium ore from 1945 through 1988. The nuclear industry dug the world's largest underground or deep uranium mine, sited by Mount Taylor. That mountain is *Tsoodzil* in the Navajo language: the sacred mountain of the south. Navajo people had no say about the desecration of that sacred place by mining.

Mining created a boomtown environment, with all its associated violence. Mining took place throughout the Navajo Nation, and as of today, there are at least one thousand abandoned and unreclaimed uranium mines within the Navajo Nation. We have not yet discovered the extent of toxic waste that came from the mills and plants that processed uranium and other products. In the aftermath of the atomic warfare and energy industry, people talk about using Indian lands to store nuclear waste.

Today, we celebrate the winning of the Cold War after the collapse of the former Soviet Union. What is the "peace dividend" for Navajo people? It is both direct and indirect.

The Victims of *Leetso*

Hundreds of Navajos worked in the open-pit and underground mines. No one told them about the dangers of radiation, so Navajo miners are dying of radiation-related diseases. They leave widows, children, and other dependents, who most often must fight hard to get compensation benefits. Many are denied compensation by a bureaucracy that is bizarre to Navajo thought. The United States Department of Justice delays and quibbles about whether widows were "married" to men who fathered children and made homes with them, making Navajo women the "tag-along" victims of radiation poisoning. These are the direct victims of the death industry that "hot" and "cold" war created.

The Navajo people use earth to build the traditional hogans—log-and-earth structures. In modern times, they use building blocks and concrete containing soil. Today, there are many Navajo homes and schools that are contaminated with radioactivity and radioactive gases. No one warned and no one cared about the waste left behind from the mines. Children play on the tailings left from a thousand or more mining sites, and strong winds blow radioactive dust across Navajo lands.

The people of the American Southwest were not told of the possible effects of bomb testing. Bombs were tested in the New Mexico and Arizona deserts near Indian nations, and an underground blast took place near the Jicarilla Apache Reservation in 1967. We are told that American servicemen were not warned or protected during atomic tests, and that there may be many communities in Nevada or New Mexico that will suffer the aftereffects of nuclear testing. The Indians who live in those areas receive America's worst health care. Even if others are tested for radiation illness, will anyone care enough to think of Indian victims?

In 1979, the retaining dam at the Church Rock mine near Gallup, New Mexico, broke, sending tons of radioactive waste down the main drainage of the area—the Rio Puerco. Cleanup operations are still going on. That disaster devastated the traditional Navajo grazing country. Navajo people could not market their meat or wool. And during the 1993 hantavirus mania over Navajo deaths, the public victimized the Navajos who lived downstream from the spill all over again.

Navajo people have a sense of humor: instead of Spider-Man—a superhero who contracted supernatural powers from radiation—the Navajo people have Mutton Man. He is said to have gotten his superhero power of flight from eating contaminated mutton from the Church Rock spill. These are the direct impacts of mining and radiation, but we sometimes forget to consider their indirect effects.

What else did the uranium industry bring to the Navajo people? Historians identify World War II as a turning point in Navajo life. Before the war, they still were able to enjoy their traditional grazing economy. The war brought Navajo people into the war industry, and the postwar energy boom forced them into the modern wage economy.

Energy development in the West created what they call the "Gillette Syndrome," after the big mining operations near Gillette, Wyoming. The boomtown atmosphere that follows energy development also fosters crime, alcoholism, child abuse, and domestic violence. Something similar happened to Navajo people. The uranium mines and mills near Navajo communities required workers. Most often they were semiskilled, and they came from rural communities. Rural Navajos live in family and clan groups, where everyone is related to, or knows everyone else. Jobs attract people who are not related to each other, and Navajo people who had previously lived in scattered rural communities were thrown together in clustered villages and towns. Women were taken from the protection of their families, quarrels over wages promoted family fights, and the sudden availability of alcohol (near the dry Navajo Nation) escalated violence. A study of Navajo families near Shiprock, New Mexico, showed that Navajo women were left unprotected in arrangements that fostered family violence.

Perhaps we should call what happened the "Shiprock Syndrome"; we could name it after the modern Navajo community near the Four Corners. Urbanization and industrial growth created what James and Elsie Zion (in their paper on domestic violence under Navajo common law) call "a climate of institutionalized violence." The secondary effects of uranium and other mineral development include alcohol-related crime, family disruption, and dependence on a wage economy that comes and goes. The traditional Navajo economy was disrupted by energy development, as was traditional family life. Abused children and brutalized women are as much the victims of atomic energy as others who suffer and die as the direct result of the atomic bomb.

Slaying the Monster

Navajo traditions are a part of their daily life. When Navajo people have practical discussions of today's problems, they often recite their sacred traditions, their sacred scripture. Navajo traditions speak of what to do with monsters such as *Leetso*.

In ancient times, Navajo people were destroyed by monsters that roamed their traditional lands. In those days, the deity Changing Woman gave birth to the Hero Twins. The Twins went through many trials and gained much wisdom from supernatural beings to acquire the skills to kill the monsters. Ironically, the first monster the Twins slew was *Yeetso*—"Big Monster." He was the biggest and the worst of the monsters, and he roamed Mount Taylor, where the world's largest underground uranium mine would be built.

Navajo thought is directly relevant to any discussion of the nuclear culture. Changing Woman, who bore and raised the Hero Twins, is also our Mother Earth. She is important to us as our Mother. As the Earth, she must not be disrespected or harmed in any way. There is an ancient Navajo belief that people should not dig into the earth—particularly with steel tools or machines. There is a story about the Hopis (retold by Frank Waters), who have a similar belief: One day, an Anglo man asked a Hopi about it. "What would happen if someone dug into the earth with a steel shovel?" he asked. The Hopi answered, "I don't know, but that would certainly tell us what kind of man he was." Sometimes we—as Indians—have a difficult time understanding the abuse of either our environment or other people.

There is another story that tells us what Navajos would have thought had they known about the use of their yellow dirt for the atom bomb. Barry Tolkein tells us of his experiences when he lived in the Navajo Nation in an essay entitled "Seeing with a Native Eye: How Many Sheep Will It Hold?" He came to know an elderly Navajo man who had never been outside the Navajo Nation. The man could not speak English or read. He did not have television, and had no other means to know anything about people other than Navajo people. Tolkein decided to educate him about the marvels and miracles of the Anglo world: He showed the man a picture of the Empire State Building in New York City. The man's reaction? "How many sheep will it hold?" Tolkein showed a picture of an airplane, and again the reaction was, "How many sheep will it hold?" The Navajo elder's reaction to the outside world was obviously framed by what he knew and held dear.

One day, as the two were talking about the wonders of the non-Navajo world, an airplane passed over. Tolkein pointed up to the vapor trail, which traced a line across the sky. The event took place during the period of atomic hysteria, when B-52 bombers formed a shield over the United States. Tolkein explained what a bomber was, relating it to the earlier picture of an airplane, and said that it carried a destructive weapon that could kill thousands of people at once. That angered the elder, who forbade any future discussion of the outside world. He was disgusted with the immoral thought that any human would kill another. The thought of thousands of people dying at the hands of another was so horrible that the elder wanted no further mention of such an immoral act.

What would the elder have said had Tolkein explained uranium and atomic energy to him? Today, many Navajo people are using their traditional ideas to discuss it. There is a Navajo saying that one should "always beware of powerful beings." A "powerful being" includes any force that we do not understand well. If we do not know it—if we cannot control it or "name" it—then it may be dangerous. One example of a powerful being we must take great care with is electricity. Although we have used it in our homes for a long time, we still do not know much about what it might do to us. The same holds true with uranium and things associated with it. It is a powerful being, and we did not take enough care to know it before attempting to use it. Anglos have another way of putting it. They say, "You have a tiger by the tail," or "You have a wolf by the tail."

There is no question that uranium is a powerful being—that it stands in the way of a successful life and therefore is a monster. How do you slay or weaken a monster? First, you know it. You must gain knowledge of its destructive force to understand what it does to you and what you can do to it. Knowledge of it is the key to knowing how to weaken or destroy it.

Second, know its fellow monsters. When an evil is done, many monsters are born of that act. Our traditions tell us that the monsters of the past were created when people transgressed, when they committed evil. The other monsters are a war industry built on disrespect for human life, and a modern international energy industry built on disrespect for both other humans and the environment. Those monsters feed on power—political power as well as nuclear power. Their nourishment comes from disrespect for the Five-Fingered People (i.e., humans), and for Mother Earth.

Third, use appropriate weapons. If the monster feeds on disrespect and abuses of power, use respect and group action as weapons. In Navajo thought, coercion is evil. We use solidarity with others and consent within the group to fight it. We use prayer and good thought to overcome coercion, which is a form of witchcraft. Put another way, we must reinforce the thought and morality of a strong international community to gain the political force necessary to counterbalance the international nuclear industry. Too often, people forget the importance of the environment to native peoples. As the World Commission on the Environment pointed out, native peoples and their thought may be a key to the future. We must be enlisted as part of a community of understanding and conscience. What we think must be part of the strategy to combat and control the monsters.

Fourth, we must have a plan. Navajo people believe that powerful forces can be controlled through understanding, and planning for group action. Navajo people did that many times in keeping the Spanish away from Navajo territory, and in coping with modern American ways. One of the things writers say often about Navajo people is that they have a canny way of taking the best from outsiders and rejecting that which does not fit the Navajo way of life. We think we can all share the approaches that Navajo and other native peoples have developed to address these issues.

Approach and Conclusion

Our thoughts are coming together as a world community: people are discussing the concept of "Gaia," the planet as a living thing that requires our respect. "Rainbow Serpent," an international women's network opposed to the destructive force of nuclear power, takes its name from the teaching of the First Nations of Australia—"Let the Rainbow Serpent sleep under the ground." Native peoples awaken to what is done to them. Their teachings may be the ancient wisdom of all people. It may be that we are all "native peoples."

In September of 1992, native or indigenous peoples met at Salzburg, Austria, to hold the World Uranium Hearing. Its final communiqué, which is dated September 19, 1992, gives us recommendations about what to do with *Leetso*. We repeat them here:

1. No more exploitation of lands and people by uranium mining, nuclear-power generation, nuclear testing, and radioactive waste dumping.
2. Clean up and restore all homelands.
3. End the secrecy and fully disclose all information about nuclear industry and its dangers.
4. Provide full and fair compensation for damage to peoples, families, and communities; cultures and economies; homelands, water, air, and all living things.
5. Provide independent and objective monitoring of human health and well-being of all living things affected by the nuclear chain.

The communiqué also reported the vision of native peoples for the future:

1. In view of the unity of humanity and the world, we appeal on behalf of future generations to use sustainable, renewable, and life-enhancing energy alternatives.
2. We call on the whole world, in particular leaders and scientists, to share in our vision for peace, harmony, and respect for life.

We support these recommendations. Nuclear power must be recognized for what it really is—a power that comes from abuse. It is the symbol of the ultimate disrespect of modern industrial society for that which native societies keep dear: Mother Earth and the Five-Fingered People. The abuse of power is tyranny, and as all modern people have done, we must fight it as a monster.

Chapter Two

"I HAVE REVISITED THE PLACES WHERE I USED TO WORK"

ORAL HISTORY OF FORMER MINER GEORGE TUTT*

Interview in Navajo by Timothy Benally, December 1995
Translation/transcription by Esther Yazzie-Lewis
and Timothy Benally

The interview that follows is with George Tutt. Mr. Tutt resides in Shiprock, New Mexico, where he has lived since 1961. He was born on October 5, 1932, and raised in Oak Springs, Arizona.

BENALLY: *We will be asking questions about uranium. When was the day that you first started working for the uranium mine?*

TUTT: When I first went to work with the uranium mining—I am kind of mixed up in years—but I think I started in 1949. This first mine where I worked in was in Colorado. It was close

---

* This article was originally published as "Into the nuclear age as a hand mucker: Interview with Navajo George Tutt, former uranium miner" in *New Solutions: A Journal of Environmental and Occupational Health Policy* 9, no. 2 (1999): 195–206. Reprinted with permission from Baywood Publishing Company, Inc.

Fig. 2.1 George Tutt Sr., Oak Springs, 1995. Photographed by Doug Brugge, courtesy of the Navajo Nation Museum, Window Rock, AZ, Catalog #URC-011.G.

to the state line, where Utah and Colorado come together. That area is called La Sal. It is near La Sal Mountain. And my first time at this mine, the mine was called Yellow Bird. I started working for VCA, Vanadium Corporation of America.

BENALLY: *What was your work? Was it in the mine?*

TUTT: I worked in the mine as what we used to call a "hand mucker." We shoveled uranium waste and uranium ore by hand. We mainly did underground mining. Wheelbarrow and shovel and pick. Most of the time that is what we did, but there were other men who worked as drillers. They drilled to make the tunnel, blasting.

BENALLY: *What really led you into uranium mining?*

TUTT: Like I say, I am from Oak Springs. Around 1930, late '30s, they started. One time, one year, there were some Anglo and Navajo people coming out to the Oak Springs area. They were observing things in Salt Canyon, when I used to herd sheep around that time. I guess they were looking for this, what they call vanadium. I guess later on they came for uranium. But this mining company was named Vanadium Corporation of America, so in those years it was men sometimes that I observed working around the edge of the cliff. At first the uranium was showing from the outside surface; later it went underground as they worked. I use to herd sheep out in that area and watch the men work. In those days they already had a jackhammer. And I used to see that the Navajo workers did not wear any safety things, like steel-toe shoes or any kind of protection against mining. Some of them were wearing moccasins.

They drilled rock, you know, from the outside surface. I guess you call it open-pit mining. When they first started, there was no protection of any kind. You know, like a mask or anything. They did not use water to drill. They just blow, as they drill, they just blow the dry rock right in their face mostly, you know. They were just covered with dust. And I watched them do that kind of work for a while. I assumed that it was work to get money to support them. My dad started with those early men, you know, working in the mine. My father's name was King Tutt...and through them, that company that was out there, through them, you know, when they needed some men out there in Colorado. So, I volunteered. I was quite young, you know. I'll say I was, I don't know, fifteen, sixteen years old.

BENALLY: *You were still a young man?*

TUTT: Yeah, yes. I remember there was a rodeo at *Tsé Dijol*, some time back, a long time ago. At that time they were working there. They mined around that area of *Tsé Dijol*. Back then, Sam Harvey and others who worked there had a rodeo. That is the only way to remember that year. Yes, I was quite young. I went to the railroad to work, before that. That is where I first got my Social Security, you know. When I went to Nebraska to work on the railroad. That is why I have a different Social Security number than the other Navajos from this area.

BENALLY: *When you worked down in the mines, what were the conditions like?*

TUTT: This question that you just asked...we were taken to Naturita. Back then there were no paved roads. Just dirt roads.

A number of us—I know Kee Begay, Jack George, and Junior George, and then myself, and I think John Pete from Mitten Rock. The five of us were taken there, to work in the mine. But we did not directly go there, but about three miles below Naturita. There was a mill, where the ore was hauled to. We worked there about two weeks. At that time, there were not too many homes. We slept under the trees there, on the slopes of the hills among the trees. I think it was in May. It was May, because it was not cold. So, we worked in the mill for two weeks.

That was what was called uranium! The filtering was done with fire underneath and it was spread out. It was pure yellow. We hauled it with wheelbarrows; that's how we worked among them. I guess it was called "uranium." We [Navajo people] call it *leetso*. That is what we did. Later, when they brought all the mining tools together, then they transported us over there. We [Navajo people] called it Five Mountains. La Sal Mountain was close by, not too far. It was that way over there too, dirt roads among the rock cliffs. A Caterpillar [construction vehicle] had graded roads . . . We were taken there in a dump truck. When we got there, we started from the outside. Uranium veins showed outside the rock ridges. We only kept after the vein. Soon we were into the rock cliff. Pretty soon, we built tunnels and hauled it [uranium] out. We used wheelbarrows, shovels, and picks. They were the only tools we used. Gloves and other tools were not available back then.

BENALLY: *Did you use a jackhammer?*

TUTT: Yes, we had that . . . Air and a jackhammer were brought over for us. That was the only way to make the hole [in the Earth]. Without it, it was impossible. Also, we used dynamite. That is where I learned what had to be done to operate a mine. I used dynamite and a jackhammer, and we experimented with this and we learned. That is the way we worked.

BENALLY: *So, when you first went to work there, was there any information about the dangers of this, and were there any safety devices given to you?*

TUTT: None. Even over here, when my father operated a mine. He never said that he was ever told about uranium. No, he never said that. It was good! Work was available close to home. We were blessed, we thought. Railroad jobs were available only far off like Denver...But for mining, one can just walk to it in the canyon. We thought we were very fortunate, but we were not told, "Later on this will affect you in this way." True, the men worked. When work stopped at the end of the shift, they just got out of the mines and went straight home. They were not told to wash or anything like that. It was like that even in Colorado—we were not told the ore might harm us. When elements are dangerous to health, signs are usually posted announcing the hazard. There were none at that time. Just worked to make money. "Got a good job and may work for a while": this is what we thought. That happened at that time.

BENALLY: *How many years did you work in the mines?*

TUTT: After I started working, and I worked later over here, in the Oak Springs area. I worked in several places in that area. Also, in Colorado again after several years, because the mines here were depleted. So, I went back to Colorado and when the jobs depleted again, then I went on to Utah—a place called Green River. And south from there, about 60 miles from there, was a rock ridge, is where we worked. There we worked a straight two-and-a-half years. All this added together, it must be about nine years...To go somewhere else for work was not thought of because this was close by. Back then we called it "good work." Good earnings were $2.50 an hour. Before that, when I first came to work, we earned something like $1 and something, I do not quite remember. And when it was around 1960, we were earning $2.50 an hour, and that was good earnings. I guess back then money was worth more, and that is why it was that way. That is the way it was.

BENALLY: *During the time when you were working, was there a time when you got sick from it, the uranium?*

TUTT: Direct injuries, there were none. Just machinery used to haul the ore out, they called it a "scoop creep." We would haul one ton of ore with it. It operated with a diesel engine. One of these crushed me. It crushed me against a rock, but that's what happened. I don't remember when it was. That was the only injury I sustained, but I was not injured bad. There was nothing that really affected my health. No.

But some years later, I started to experience some respiratory problems. It was obvious, because I was short of breath when I walked up hills. I would get sweaty and short of breath. The health examinations traced the problem back to mining, and it has affected me. It is still the same today. In the beginning it was slight, but I was not aware of it then; but it became obvious later on. I used to go hunting a lot. I don't do that anymore. It has been like that for several years now. Now, I experience shortness of breath. Even when I talk, I talk like I'm stuttering. That is how it is now.

BENALLY: *How do you feel about the mining that took place and your work at the uranium mills? What do you think of that now?*

TUTT: As I think of it now, I have revisited the places where I used to work not too long ago. In fact, it was just over a week ago. At Naturita there is a place called Long Park, and it is a long rock ridge. That was the area where work was really done. It was about 30 years ago when I first worked [there]. I wanted to find out the name of the mine, but there was no one who I could ask, because they have died off. I worked with five or six people—some looked young, and yet they are gone. There were some older ones, too. So, the only thing to do was to go back to where I used to work; that is why I revisited the site. It was hard to find anything, if there was still an office or they are gone, but I made an attempt to find out.

I might meet someone, I thought. Immediately, I was fortunate when I got to Naturita. There is a white man who lives over the hill, a place called Nucla, Colorado. When I inquired at a restaurant, they said his name was Pat Daniel. They said he knew all about the mines around there...and that he had become quite old now. Then I proceeded to visit him, and they were right about him. He was also living alone, and his relatives had died off. He brought out a big map. He had all the names of the mines on the map. I told him that I worked here on the map, Uravan, and in between near the rock ridge. There were many mines close together and the names were there.

I remember a mine call Vanadium King; there were Navajo people working there that I knew. They used to work there, and I used that name in order to find out where it was. The name was "Donald L.," that was the name of the mine. I inquired about some of the white men I worked with, and he told me they died, so many years ago. I thought that maybe one of the white men might remember the name of the mine, but they were also all gone. So, it was difficult, but this white man had a map and that is how I was able to obtain the name. He had worked with all the companies, like VCA and Union Carbide... and he worked at the mill here at Shiprock, too. He knew some of the Navajo people who worked there. He was the boss, at times...

Some of the mines have been closed up [sealed], but where I worked the mine is still open. The mine had an incline where the small rail cars would haul out the ore... The main reason for getting the name of the mine was because they were measuring the uranium activity at these mines. Where we worked, we worked with nothing but the yellow ore. We would find these [yellow strips]—like you found big dead snakes, because you could see where the head was and the tail was. When you dynamited the wall of the rock ridge, you could see it. We would look at it and wonder what it was. We would say it must have been the ancient monster snakes from the beginning of time. The strips [veins] were yellow, bare yellow. They said it was called "high grade." We were not even afraid of it; it was work and we were getting paid. We would go home and back to visit our relatives, and we would haul back food. That is what we did when we worked. So, when I went back to revisit the site, I was remembering these people and it made me feel bad [emotional] for them.

BENALLY: *It was the United States government whose money was used for uranium, and the Navajo people worked—Navajo uranium miners, and some white people and Mexicans. The United States government worked with the Navajo people—are they given fair treatment, today?*

Fig. 2.2 Miner riding small rail car. Kerr McGee Oil Industries Inc., Navajo Uranium Mine near Cove, Arizona, 1952. Photographed by Milton Snow, courtesy of the Navajo Nation Museum, Window Rock, AZ, Catalog #NG6–52.

Tutt: I do not know if I will be answering correctly. Now there are things like compensation available [the Radiation Exposure Compensation Act of 1990—eds.] . . . I do not think it was worth it. Even if they say $100,000, because white folks wanted paybacks and they get big bucks, millions. This one hundred thousand is nothing. It is very little. Some of them have not fully understood this, what is called "fair treatment." It is far from it.

Benally: *Okay, next . . . this thing called compensation, which you made mention of, how can this be made so the people will receive it? Can you talk about this?*

Tutt: There was a time from the beginning when the men did not work with precautions. There was nothing about safety. And when we got married and we had children, they were all exposed to it. At that time, the only way was to wash by hand. The clothes we worked in were washed at home; there were no laundromats. We did not know anything like that, back then. So they were exposed. It was in those years when the men were seriously affected that way. They were not told of how they should take care of themselves...

It was not until some time later that baths and washing came to be, and they also talked about it...But, if they had been teaching at the time, it would have been good...They never said it would kill us. If this had been brought to their attention immediately, back then, many of them probably would have left it...Now, it is hard to tell. We do not know how long some of them worked.

They [the U. S. government] are not even complying with the laws [RECA] which were made. So, some of the miners died of different things, like vehicle accidents, and they are gone. Back then, they did not go to the hospitals. There are no records, even of x-rays. There is nothing. So I do not know about that. And because of unclear records, I'm sure some were paid; [compensation claims] need to be processed in a better manner. There are some [processes] which are time consuming. This is how it was for some. That is how it is with the compensation part. It is confusing, but it is probably good, too. And some of them got some money. There are many men who have died off and are survived by their children. They [miners] did not see [the money].

I would like to talk about a specific thing here, regarding this questioning. It would have been good to apply without attorneys. The 10 percent [paid to lawyers] seemed like money taken away from the people without reason. This money was a gift. Instead, the attorneys got involved and they took most of the money. The money was for the uranium miners. The cause was for the miners' families, and I really disapprove of the [attorney fees] they took from them. When they were making the legislation, they should have made it so that the people got all of the money, because they were the ones who did the work...But as I look at it, it seems you have to practically be dead in order for your papers to be forwarded. That's the way it has been. There are some [lawyers] who work diligently on their compensation, and there are others who don't have to work so hard for it...

BENALLY: *In the future, if they say they want to do uranium mining again, how do you feel about this?*

TUTT: I don't know how it will be. I don't know. If there was a demand for it, perhaps it will be done in some way. To this day, there are many new tools being developed. The past mining experiences we know were not good, not right, and if the same employment is used, it will be repeated. Kill more people. Teaching and modern equipment [might help].

BENALLY: *Next... the families that were exposed to uranium, what you brought up. Maybe one of your children might have been told, "This is affecting them"?*

TUTT: Regarding the spouses, back then we had just met each other. It was that way with the young men that I worked with. The women folks were exposed through washing clothes; that is the way it was. So, when we lived at the mine sites, some of us just lived in tents. The tents were small, like the ones they use to set up camp when they're herding sheep... The spouses were really exposed. The children were also exposed, especially the older ones. They were exposed.

If you're exposed, it would not affect you until later on. There are some who are equally affected... Some are affected immediately and others not until later. But then, I don't know, when there is a husband and wife who were exposed and it became a part of their system, will their offspring be affected in the future, too? All these things need to be researched, and I hear this was being done and they examined us. We have children who are like that. They are slow at learning. They have a mental deficiency. Can that be caused by uranium? If it is in your system, it will do that to a child. Maybe they are still researching that, I do not know. I know that.

BENALLY: *Who was doing the research?*

TUTT: Wasn't it Lora Shields? A woman, named Dr. Lora Shields. She really examined us, just like this, by interviewing us...[1]

BENALLY: *Yes, we know about that and we will look at it... There is uranium waste and abandoned mines on Navajo land. There is waste left exposed on the surface, and there is reclamation being done. There is one over there who is doing that. Do you think this is beneficial? Are they doing a good job covering it up, or are they not doing a good job?*

TUTT: At one time I wanted to know how it was being done, and I made a visit to one of the sites. I saw that it was done right. When it is hauled, it is piled up in one place. If some of the waste should spread out, then it is easier to clean up. There are some that have been hidden again [buried]... That is good. The mines that are out in the bad land, the mine holes are deep and there are big, deep drops. Therefore, it is difficult to completely cover up the waste, unachievable. The mines have tunnels and roads; maybe they can recover them in those areas, then maybe it is workable. Then it would be a job well done. When you have an open area with easy access, then it is not hard to do, but when you mined in the crevices of the mountains, it is hard to cover those areas. There is too much left uncovered. This is risky and difficult. That is how it is. Also...

BENALLY: *Okay. Oh, go ahead.*

TUTT: It has been several years. There are some places where I did mining where there are still uncovered mines; for example, I said I went to revisit the area in Naturita. Where I mined, the mine is left open; the other mines around are covered up. So it varies. Now, if they covered up all the area at the same time, then it would be good. But they cover some and not others. There are other areas where the hole went straight down, where they were elevated up and down, that is easy; but the waste which was taken out and piled up is still there. No one is doing anything about it. That is how it is.

BENALLY: *Next... from back then to what it is today, people worked in uranium mines and many people were affected by it. And even though there is some compensation, a person will sometimes say, "I would like to be remembered by this," if a person has some idea or plans for the people to be recognized* *by. A person may say, "This is what I think." What would you say to your grandchildren or great grandchildren?*

TUTT: What I think is there is only one thing. This thing called uranium is very dangerous. That is what it is called. If inhaled, it will affect you inside. You have to beware of the danger. I am sure there is good money in the work, but if you compare life with money, money is nothing. It is not worth much, is how I think. The Five-Fingered people, humanity, is priceless. If there is something to be remembered—it is better not to work with uranium. If you are going to take the risk and work with uranium, then you need to wear some safety clothes. Then it would be good. To just work without any safety clothes and tools is not worth it. Because you would be giving up your life. That is how it is. Warning: it is better that people do not work with [uranium]. It would require working in safety clothes and shoes. That would be good.

BENALLY: *The last one: What did you think about what we have questioned you about, and if there is anything you feel you were not asked about, you can talk about it. That will finish the questioning.*

TUTT: This question, there are many things to be said. These questions just cover certain areas. But it is good. When you are being questioned, then a person tends to forget things to be said. There are many people who died. When I am being questioned, it is emotional. When you think of the men you worked with, some were young. They were not even 40 years old. They have died. So, there are different variations. One thing that I have to say is that it is not worth it. Maybe in the future it may be worth it, mentally. That is how it is. But I do not know how that works. I do not know about our spouses and children and how they are affected by it. They need to be paid for their exposure separately, too. They have health problems, too, with their respiration. That much I would like to say to complete this.

BENALLY: *Okay. Thank you for your time and answers. I do know something about the people's problems. I do work with the people, and when I tell others, they do not believe me. They say, "You're the only one saying this." When you can name a person to say, "This is what they said," then there is a foundation to what is being said. There will be documentation. That is the reason. Thank you, my friend, for talking with us.*

TUTT: In regard to this questioning, if this will help my fellow miners, then it will be good. When I am asked to talk about this and it is not going to be used, then it is not worth it. If it is good for the people...half of the miners are still living. They are not all gone. Now, if there are safety measures taken, then it would be good. If these questionings are put into documentation and then not used, it is not good; it would not be good for anything. Now, if it is used for supporting and forcing the process of compensation, making it possible, then it is good. Then it would be good there were interviews. That is how I think of it.

BENALLY: *Okay.*

Notes

1.   L. M. Shields, W. H. Wiese, B. J. Skipper, B. Charley, L. Benally, Navajo birth outcomes in the Shiprock uranium mining area, *Health Phys* 63 (1992): 542–51.

Chapter Three

A DOCUMENTARY HISTORY OF URANIUM MINING AND THE NAVAJO PEOPLE*

Doug Brugge and Rob Goble

In 1990 the U.S. Congress passed the Radiation Exposure Compensation Act (hereafter RECA, Public Law 101–426, 1990). The act acknowledged responsibility for the historical mistreatment of uranium miners by the U.S. government, the sole purchaser of uranium from 1948 to 1971 (Eichstaedt 1994; ACHRE 1995; Moure-Eraso 1999), and made provision for financial compensation to miners with diseases that could be related to their mining experience. Ten years later (June 2000), the U.S. Congress passed, and the president signed, legislation amending the original law to correct for what were widely perceived as areas of unfairness in the original legislation (hereafter RECA Amendments) (Woolf 2000).

In this chapter, we recount the history of U.S. uranium mining leading to the 1990 RECA. Chapter 10 discusses the aftermath of the 1990 RECA. The 100-year legacy of deaths from uranium mining spanning the European and the U.S.

* This article was originally published as "The history of uranium mining and the Navajo People" in the *American Journal of Public Health* 92 (2002): 1410–19. Reprinted with permission from the American Public Health Association.

experiences, the 30-year struggle to obtain reparations, the controversy following passage of the 1990 RECA, as well as the debate over amending RECA, all raise critical questions about how to protect workers, how to compensate those who become ill, and the tradeoff between national security and the environmental health of workers and communities. Our perspective for examining this history is the Navajo experience. We chose this approach because we are more familiar with the Navajo experience than that of white and Hispanic miners, because environmental justice encourages a look at the environmental experience of minority communities (Institute of Medicine 1999; Bullard 1994), because minority miners are among the least-advantaged populations with respect to workplace safety (Cherniack 1996), and perhaps most importantly, because Navajo uranium activists themselves have been at the forefront of advocating for compensation and justice, and we are fortunate to be able to draw directly upon their knowledge and experience (Eichstaedt 1994).

The Early European Experience

Prior to the U.S. nuclear program, uranium-bearing ore had been mined for centuries in Schneeberg (Germany) and Jachimov (Czechoslovakia) for metals and the manufacture of uranium dyes. An association, long observed, between these mining activities and a lung disease, then called "Bergkrankheit," was first reported in detail in 1879 (Härting et al. n.d.; Arnstein 1913; Lorenz 1944; Holaday 1969). The investigators reported that 75 percent of all deaths among miners were due to this disease. Later follow-up (Arnstein 1913) reduced this extraordinary estimate by about a third, provided detailed histological descriptions of the cancers, and also discussed a high prevalence of nonmalignant lung disease. An imprecise retrospective estimate suggests that these miners were exposed to roughly 30–150 Working Levels (see page 31) while they were mining (Holaday 1969). In 1926, clinical evaluation defined the histopathology of the lung cancer in miners

(Lorenz 1944). By 1932, Germany and Czechoslovakia had designated cancer in these miners as a compensable occupational disease (ACHRE 1995).

The Boom in Uranium Mining in the United States

After its initial dependence on foreign sources, the U.S. Atomic Energy Commission announced in 1948 that it would guarantee a price for and purchase all uranium ore that was mined in the United States. This initiated a mining "boom" on the Colorado Plateau in New Mexico, Utah, Colorado, and Arizona that replaced a more limited mining industry centered first on radium and then vanadium, which are found in the same easy-to-mine, soft sandstone ore (Ringholtz 1989; Holaday 1969). The U.S. government remained, by law, the sole purchaser of uranium in the United States until 1971, but private companies operated the mines (Pearson 1980). Purchases of uranium by the Atomic Energy Commission (AEC) dropped in the late 1960s when the U.S. government decided it had acquired enough. Commercial purchases rose, however, to roughly replace AEC purchases by 1971, and remained strong into the 1980s (New Mexico Energy Institute 1976; USDOE 1984).

By 1958 there were 7,500 reports of uranium finds in the United States, with over 7 million tons of ore identified (Eichstaedt 1994). During the mid-1950s peak, there were about 750 mines in operation (Committee on the Biological Effects of Ionizing Radiation 1999). The Navajo Reservation (today called the Navajo Nation), situated on one corner of the uranium-mining belt, was swept into the boom, expanding from its 1944 contract with Vanadium Corporation of America for uranium production (Eichstaedt 1994). Uranium was discovered in Cove, Arizona, and then elsewhere in the reservation (Brugge et al. 1999). Eventually, four centers of mining and milling operated on reservation land near Shiprock, New Mexico (including the Carrizo Mountains, near Cove, Arizona); in Monument Valley, Utah; at Church Rock, New Mexico; and Kayenta, Arizona (see map in figure 3.1). In addition, many Navajo people traveled to

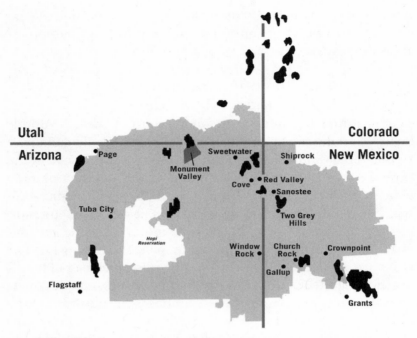

Fig. 3.1 Map of the Navajo Nation, with key towns and uranium mining areas marked in black.

mines off the reservation seeking work; they often moved their families with them and lived in mine camps (T. Benally, oral communications, 1998–1999). Uranium production in the northern and western Carrizo Mountains of the Navajo Nation began in 1948, peaked in the years 1955 and 1956, and declined to zero again by 1967 (Stern 1992; Moure-Eraso 1999). More than 1,000 abandoned uranium mine shafts are now estimated to lie on Navajo land (P. Charley, oral communication, 1995).

The Navajo People at the Start of Uranium Mining

Navajo men gravitated to work in the mines, which was about the only job available near to home (see figure 3.2). For many Navajo families, uranium mining represented a first contact with the broader U.S. wage economy. These Navajo families

Fig. 3.2 Navajo miners dumping low-grade ore. Kerr McGee Oil Industries Inc., Navajo Uranium Mine near Cove, Arizona, July 23, 1952. Photographed by Milton Snow, courtesy of the Navajo Nation Museum, Window Rock, AZ, Catalog # NG6–67.

were thankful at the time that they had employment (Brugge and Benally 1998; Brugge et al. 1999).

Miners were paid minimum wage or less. Copies of pay stubs provided by a Navajo miner from 1949 show an hourly salary of $0.81–$1.00 (D. Crank, written communication, 1998). The positions that they held included blasters, timber men (building the wooden supports in the mines), muckers (who dug the blasted rock), transporters, and millers. Navajo miners report that the bosses were usually white, and that the foremen did not spend as much time in the mines as did the Navajo laborers. Mining tools ranged from pickax and wheelbarrow to heavy equipment. Navajo workers reported working as little as a few months to 10 years or more in uranium mines (Eichstaedt 1994; Brugge et al. 1997).

When uranium mining began, the dominant modes of transportation for Navajo people were by horse and wagon or by foot on the reservation; the Navajo language had no word for *radiation*, few Navajos spoke English, and few had formal education. Thus, the Navajo population was isolated from the general flow of knowledge about radiation and its hazards by geography, language, and literacy level (Eichstaedt 1994; Brugge et al. 1997). Today, the miners and their families say that they had no idea that there were long-term health hazards associated with uranium mining. Virtually all of the Navajo miners report that they were not educated about the hazards of uranium mining and were not provided with protective equipment or ventilation (Dawson, 1992).

Today, many Navajo people note that the Treaty of 1868 between the Navajo Tribe (now the Navajo Nation) and the U.S. government assigned the Bureau of Indian Affairs to care for Navajo economic, education, and health services. They view this as a special trust relationship that carried particular responsibilities, including safeguarding the health of the Navajo people (Brugge et al. 1997). However, government-provided health care for Navajo people has been fraught with problems. From the 1800s through the 1940s, it focused more on eliminating the role of native healers, or medicine men, than on curing widespread infectious disease. Thus uranium-mining-related disease arose in a context of other public-health failures (Tennert and Litchford 1998).

The Causal Agent for Lung Cancer in Uranium Miners Is Identified in the Early 1950s

Although unknown to the Navajo people, by the late 1930s there was no scientific doubt that uranium mining was associated with high rates of lung cancer (Peller 1939). The debate turned to identifying the causal agent. Clear evidence that policy makers thought that radon was involved came from a ventilation project begun in Joachimsthal, Czechoslovakia, by the Ministry of Public Works in 1930. This effort was reported to have reduced radon from unventilated levels of 320–8,950 pCi/L (0.32–8.9 WL) to below 350 pCi/L (0.35 WL) by use of ventilation (Behounek 1970).

A 1942 review by Wilhelm Hueper (1942) suggested that radiation was the causal agent. A 1944 review by Egon Lorenz (1944), however, concluded that radiation could not be the causal agent since x-rays giving doses comparable to those from the radon gas did not have the same effect in animals. This was correct, but as was shown later, an incomplete analysis. Scientific opinion in the mid-1940s was not clear, and was somewhat divided as to the agent responsible for elevated lung-cancer rates among uranium miners.

Finally, work by William Bale and John Harley, based on Harley's 1952 PhD dissertation (Harley 1952, 1953) resolved the question of how radon could cause such high rates of lung cancer. Bale reported in an influential memorandum (Bale 1980) that it was the radon-daughter isotopes that contributed the bulk of the radiation to the lung. Unlike radon gas, the radon daughters can be retained in the lung adjacent to sensitive cells for periods of time as long as their radioactive half-lives, delivering high doses of alpha radiation. This explanation, coincident with the expansion of uranium mining in the United States, was a singular achievement since the causal links of few other toxins were understood at that time.

Measuring Radon in the Mines

Early measurements were of the concentration of radon in the air in mines—typically measured in picocuries per liter (pCi/L). Harley's work focused on the radon daughters and led to the definition of a Working Level (WL) as the measure of the energy released by radon daughters. This provides a physical measure that is closely related to the mechanism for biological damage. One WL is a concentration of radon-decay products that will release 1.3 million electron volts per liter of air. Depending on ventilation and the amount of dust, a particular concentration of radon in the air can correspond to different values of WL (Committee on the Biological Effects of Ionizing Radiation 1988). At equilibrium, which is expected with poor ventilation, one WL corresponds to 100 pCi/L in air. The commonly reported measure of exposure depends on both the amount of radioactivity and duration, and is called a "Working Level Month" or WLM. One WLM is equal to spending 170 hours (one month of working hours) exposed to one WL.

The Public Health Service Study

In 1950 the U.S. Public Health Service (PHS) began a study of uranium miners in the Colorado Plateau, based on concerns that the European experience implied that radon in U.S. mines would cause lung cancer (ACHRE 1995; Archer et al. 1962; Lundin et al. 1971; NIOSH 1987; Donaldson 1969). The study measured both radon in mines and health outcomes, i.e., lung cancer. The study failed to inform miners of the risks being studied (ACHRE 1995) and initially focused its attention on white miners, although the first full report did report mortality for the nonwhite population as well (Lundin et al. 1971). In the 1980s, Jonathan Samet and collaborators made a full analysis of the Navajo population (Samet et al. 1988).

Victor Archer, who led the PHS medical team, has been quoted as saying, "We did not want to rock the boat...We had to take the position that we were neutral scientists trying to find out what the facts were, that we were not going to make any public announcements until the results of our scientific study were completed" (Ball 1993, 46). There were some pamphlets that mentioned a risk of lung cancer given to miners in 1959, but they minimized the level of concern (ACHRE 1995), and it is unclear how widely these materials were disseminated, or what was the literacy/English comprehension of the miners who received them.

The PHS protocol is ethically troubling. The centerpiece of the Nuremberg Code, promulgated in 1947 and widely publicized, was provision of informed consent to persons enrolled in research studies. The PHS study clearly violated a central tenet of the standard of care of the time, as well as the standards of today. Notably, the uranium-miner study also took place after the start of the better-known Tuskegee Study of black men with syphilis, which was also run by the U.S. PHS. However, the Tuskegee Study did not come to public awareness until 1972 (Rothman 1991).

Other Related Diseases

New knowledge about other health hazards of mining also emerged. Silicosis and its causes became a prominent concern after large numbers of deaths, disproportionately among black miners, at Hawks Nest, West Virginia (Cherniack 1986). Hazards of coal mining and "black lung disease" became a national concern in the mid-1960s (Smith 1987; Rosner and Markowitz 1991). Serious respiratory disease became viewed generally as a plausible hazard of mining. Furthermore, there were clear observations in the early European experience and in the PHS study that other respiratory illnesses, including silicosis, tuberculosis, pneumonia, and emphysema, were causing deaths in uranium miners at rates approaching those from lung cancer. For the Navajo cohort in the PHS study, the death rate from nonmalignant respiratory disease was essentially the same as the death rate from lung cancer (Roscoe et al. 1995).

The Response to the Hazards of Uranium Mining

Some U.S. officials and scientists advocated ventilation requirements in U.S. mines as a proactive, preventive measure during the 1950s, based on their knowledge of European experience. For instance, Duncan Holaday, an industrial hygienist with the PHS, has generally been recognized as the most prominent advocate for ventilation. He led the effort to obtain measurements of radon in the mines, and used the data to argue forcefully within the government that ventilation would be effective and was feasible (Holaday 1957). His arguments achieved only limited success, as there was government resistance to requiring ventilation and his views were not made public at the time (Archer 1990).

The Atomic Energy Commission (AEC) was an obstacle. In the late 1940s, controversy erupted in the New York Operations Office over the hazards from beryllium and uranium mining. The AEC wrote worker health requirements in contracts with companies that handled beryllium. After conflicting recommendations from staff, it chose not to establish such requirements for uranium. It claimed to lack legal authority, but did not explain the legal difference between uranium and beryllium. The AEC did not lack knowledge: records of a January 25, 1951, internal meeting of AEC and PHS staff reveal that the staff believed, based on early measurements, that radon was present in levels that would cause cancer, and that ventilation could abate the hazard. Public acknowledgment of this problem was apparently squelched. For instance, Hueper, the scientist who wrote the 1942 review, was then at the National Cancer Institute, and was forbidden to speak in public about his concerns about the health hazard of radon in uranium mines. It is reported that he was even forbidden to *travel* west of the Mississippi, lest he say too much to the wrong people (ACHRE 1995).

Education and State Efforts at Ventilation during the 1950s and 1960s

Rather than create federal requirements, federal officials tried to encourage states and mine owners to improve conditions. They conducted several public forums for mine operators and state-government officials about the hazards of uranium mining, including an early forum in 1951. A 1957 report by Holaday and colleagues (Holaday et al. 1957) laid out an approach for controlling radon in mines. They proposed a tentative threshold exposure value of one WL, but stopped short of making a definitive recommendation because of what, in hindsight, looks like an exaggerated concern about uncertainties in interpreting radon measurements. The report showed that radon concentrations in most of the 157 mines tested were above levels that required ventilation, and went on to discuss mechanical ventilation (natural ventilation was found to be insufficient). The public education efforts culminated with a presentation to the Governor's Conference (of southwestern states) in 1960. The states did adopt guidelines for radon at levels equivalent to one WL, and in 1958 New Mexico adopted a policy of clearing all areas that exceeded 10 WL. There was, however, limited enforcement of state regulations in the period before federal regulations appeared at the end of the 1960s (Eichstaedt 1994; Holaday 1969).

Levels of Radon Measured in the Mines

Depending on which measurements are considered and what credence they are given, one can draw different conclusions about the effect of state regulation. Estimates of average exposures of miners over the 1960s show only a moderate decline, which can be attributed to the gradual installation of better ventilation (BEIR VI, Annex E1). However, levels reported as a percent of measurements in excess of 10 WL declined very gradually from 1950 to 1960, fell precipitously from 1960 to 1962, and then continued a gradual decline into the 1970s (Pearson 1980). The sharp decline from 1960–1962 corresponds to the institution of government inspection and the choice by one state, New Mexico, to close mines that exceeded the 10 WL limit. It is likely that reductions in radon levels could have been largely confined to larger mines that were inspected more often and that were run by companies with more resources to install ventilation. Further, it does not necessarily follow from this record that ventilation was always used when inspectors were absent, and for many mines, there are no records at all.

Levels of radon measured in mines on the Navajo Reservation were lower. This was attributed to the mines being smaller and having better natural ventilation (Holaday 1969). It is not clear to us, however, whether the inspection rates and installation of ventilation that led to progressive declines in radon levels elsewhere were mirrored in Navajo mines.

A Statistically Significant Association

By 1959, the PHS study of U.S. uranium miners had shown that there was a statistically significant association between uranium mining and lung cancer for white miners, a result that was reported in the literature in 1962 (Archer 1962). The reason for excluding minority miners (who were included in the field study) from the analysis was apparently a scientific desire to report on a homogeneous population. The study sought mathematical precision of the association, rather than the more general fact that uranium mining led to exposure to radon, which caused lung cancer.

Later in the 1960s, it became apparent that smoking was a modifier of risk, and that most of the lung cancers in white miners were among smokers. This did not change the strong association with radon exposures, but it added a complication that coincided with the U.S. Surgeon General's 1964 report on smoking and health (USDOH 1964; Parascandola 2001), marking the key turning point in public awareness of the hazards of smoking.

The Navajo People and Smoking

A 1968 survey of cigarette use by Southwestern Native Americans (Sievers 1968) reported that only 4.4 percent of male Native Americans smoked more than one pack per day, while some 33.3 percent of the male non-Indian population smoked more than one pack per day. Today only 4 percent of Navajo men over age 60 report being current smokers (Mendlein et al. 1997). In a study of Navajo uranium miners, 58.9 percent were reported to never have been smokers. Ex-smokers and light smokers (<1 pack per day) made up 37 percent of these Navajo uranium miners (USDOH 1964).

Tobacco is used for ceremonial and cultural purposes on a regular but limited basis by much of the Navajo population. Consequently, records in which Navajo miners represent themselves as "smokers" may not refer to addictive smoking. The amount of tobacco smoked would likely be far less than one pack per year over a lifetime for most Navajos who smoke (T. Benally, oral communication, July 1998), although we know of no quantification of ceremonial smoking.

The Navajo People Begin to Organize as Illnesses Appear

By ten years of mining, the first cases of lung cancer had begun appearing in uranium miners. The affected Navajo communities looked for the cause of this heretofore rare to nonexistent disease. In the 1960s, Navajo widows came together, and they talked about their husbands' deaths and how they had died. The process that they initiated, which included steep learning curves about science, politics, and organizing, would culminate some thirty years later in the passage of RECA (Eichstaedt 1994; Brugge et al. 1997; Dawson et al. 1997). To visit the homes of the widows in Cove, Arizona, today—to see the lack of phones, the wood stoves, and remoteness of the community—is to marvel at the fact that their complaint ever reached Washington, DC. Their story is still largely oral, and unrecorded in any detail to our knowledge. However, Peter Eichstaedt (1994) relates that Harry Tome of Red Valley, a tribal council member and later employee of the minerals department of the Tribe, was one of those who noticed the problem in the early 1960s. Tome later became a leading advocate on the issue.

Federal Regulations Are Finally Established at the End of the 1960s

National regulations for uranium mining were first debated in the U.S. Congress in 1966 before the Labor Subcommittee of the Senate Committee on Labor and Public Welfare, but little attention was initially paid to the problem (Eichstaedt 1994). A story by J. V. Reistrup in the *Washington Post* in March 1967 that described the health hazards started the national news coverage (Eichstaedt 1994; Ringholtz 1989), and newspaper coverage of the issue registered a sharp peak in 1967 (Pearson 1980). This preceded the more dramatic uprising of unionized coal miners in Appalachia that climaxed in 1968–69. The coal-miner strike involved tens of thousands of miners, with prominent national coverage, and was not subject to the national-security issues that cloaked uranium mining. The coal strike led to the passage of both regulations on conditions in the mines and a compensation system for disabled coal miners (Smith 1987).

The connection between the labor unions and the Navajo miners was complex. Anthony Mazzocchi, former leader of the Oil, Chemical, and Atomic Workers International, argued before Congress that the research studies should include results for Navajo people, not just for whites, but Navajo people did not testify directly in this first congressional debate (Eichstaedt 1994). While some Navajo miners were members of unions if they worked in the many off-reservation mines, there was apparently no unionization of miners on the reservation itself (A. Mazzocchi, oral communication, March 2001). None of the miners that we spoke to recalled unions operating in reservation mines, and one of the editors of this volume recalls being fired for suggesting that the workers needed a union (T. Benally, oral communication, 2000). The Navajo Tribal Council had outlawed union activity on the reservation in 1958, and union members on the reservation numbered only 300 by 1971 (Jorgenson et al. n.d.). Thus, while the unions were a source of information and advocacy, they were not part of the organizing of Navajo people, which proceeded primarily on the reservation at the community level, far from Washington, DC.

The standard that was finally set for radon in mines, 0.3 WL, was effective January 1, 1969 (Eichstaedt 1994). It is essentially the standard that applies today, reformulated as 4 WLM/year. Mazzocchi noted in 1977 that violations of the existing standard occur even after advance notice is given to mining companies of pending inspections (Mazzocchi and Wodka 1977). In 1987 the National Institute of Occupational Safety and Health (NIOSH) proposed lowering the standard to one WLM/year, a recommendation that has yet to be implemented. NIOSH asserted that the more stringent standard was both necessary to protect health and feasible with available technology (Ball 1993).

Navajo Advocacy in the 1970s and 1980s

Tome, the early Navajo advocate, prompted the *Albuquerque Tribune* to run a cover story in 1973 that led to the first legislation in the U.S. Congress aimed at compensation. It was designed to extend black-lung benefits to uranium miners. The bill never passed, despite Tome's dogged lobbying efforts over a number of years. In 1978 Tome began working with Stuart Udall, secretary of the interior under President John F. Kennedy. Ultimately, Udall filed two lawsuits in 1979 seeking damages for uranium miners. One was aimed at the mining companies; the other was filed against the U.S. Department of Energy (Eichstaedt 1994).

Legal Challenges in the 1970s and 1980s

The case against the mining companies was thrown out of court in 1980 based on the mine-company argument that workers were covered by workers' compensation, which precludes lawsuits against the workers' employer for occupational health and safety injuries or illness (Schwartz 1988; Boden 2000). Ironically, many miners with illnesses were either denied claims under the state worker's-compensation systems, or never filed claims (Ringholtz 1989). Mining companies have largely avoided liability to date; a rare exception was a court ruling against a uranium mill in Colorado in which members of the community, rather than workers, sued for damages (Zubeck 1998).

The suit filed by Udall in federal district court in Arizona seemed a more promising route to gain compensation for uranium miners (*Begay v. US*). Udall hoped that the trust relationship of the Navajo Tribe to the United States might overcome the judicial bias in favor of federal immunity from lawsuits. However, the court ruled in 1984 that the U.S. government was immune (Udall 1994). The decision cited national security as the government's interest. The court did indicate that federal legislation would be necessary, and that the situation "cries for redress" (ACHRE 1995, 577). The Advisory Committee on Human Radiation Experiments later concluded that "there is no obvious national security or other ground on which to justify the continued exposure of miners to the radon hazard" (ACHRE 1995, 577).

Congressional Hearings on Compensation

In 1979, congressional hearings were held in Grants, New Mexico, adjacent to the Mount Taylor uranium-mining area. A large number of white and Navajo uranium miners testified, offering heartfelt and tragic stories. Leading the Navajo delegation was Tome. The legislation under consideration in 1979 was still modeled after black-lung benefits, that is, a small monthly stipend (Eichstaedt 1994). In 1980, congressional hearings considered creating an exemption to make the United States liable for damages to downwinders and uranium miners. The eligibility criterion for miners was one year of work in the mines

(RECA Hearing 1981). The hearing the following year focused on the population living downwind from the atomic bomb tests (RECA Hearing 1982). In 1982, however, Navajo people showed up in force at a Senate hearing in Salt Lake City, Utah. The Navajo attendees were last on the agenda, and Senator Orrin Hatch observed that the hearing was about fallout victims, and that worker's compensation would be taken up later. The Navajo contingent proceeded anyway, and Leo Redhouse, Sam Jones, Harold Tso, Harry Tome, Perry Charley, and Harris Charley again gave highly personal accounts of the suffering of Navajo miners, including themselves (RECA Hearing, 1982).

A Scientific Understanding of
Radon Dose Response

While organizing progressed and hearings were held in the 1980s, new information about miners, radon, and lung cancer appeared. An important secondary literature reviewed and combined studies to more precisely define the dose/response relationship. The National Academy of Sciences' Institute of Medicine, Biological Effects of Ionizing Radiation subcommittee (BEIR), conducts the major U.S. effort. BEIR IV, published in 1988 (Committee on the Biological Effects of Ionizing Radiation 1988), combined four studies of miners, the Colorado study, and studies from Newfoundland, Ontario, and Beaverlodge, Saskatchewan. BEIR IV identified a dependence of risk on time since exposure, and on attained age. The BEIR VI report, published in 1999 (Committee on the Biological Effects of Ionizing Radiation 1999), reviewed 11 studies of miners. It identified additional dependence of risk on the intensity and/or duration of exposure, and created two models—an "exposure-age-duration" model, and an "exposure-age-concentration" model—to reflect such dependence. Both BEIR IV and BEIR VI contained substantial discussion of the joint effects of radon exposure and smoking.

Smoking is a complicating factor in determining the risk of lung cancer from radon exposure among uranium miners. In the Colorado Plateau study cohort, about 84 percent of miners were either current or ex-smokers (Roscoe 1997). By the mid-1960s, it had been recognized that most of the uranium miners who developed lung cancer were smokers. BEIR IV (Committee on the Biological Effects of Ionizing Radiation 1988) suggested that smoking and radon exposure result in a greater than additive, but less than multiplicative risk of lung cancer. This conclusion was strengthened by the analysis in BEIR VI (Committee on the Biological Effects of Ionizing Radiation 1999), which included direct evidence of increased cancer incidence among never-smokers. A recent case-control study of Navajo uranium miners reports that adjustment for smoking status did not change the strong relationship between lung cancer and mining uranium (Gilliland et al. 2000).

As a result of smoking rates below those of the general population, lung-cancer rates have also remained comparatively low in Native American populations in the Southwest. Age-adjusted annual mortality rates for lung cancer among New Mexico Native Americans (which included many Navajo people) rose from 5.3 (per 100,000) in 1958–62 to 10.8 in 1978–82. By comparison, the rate for the white population rose from 38.5 to 70.4 during the same period (Samet 1988).

The rate for Navajo people may in fact be even lower than for Native Americans more generally. For 1991–93, the age-adjusted lung-cancer mortality rate for Native Americans living in the IHS-designated "Navajo area" was 4.8 (A. Handler, Indian Health Service, written communication, November 24, 1997).

Health Consequences as Learned from the Dose Response Model

It has been estimated that 500–600 of the thousands of uranium miners who worked between 1950 and 1990 died of lung cancer, that most of these deaths were associated with radon exposure, and that a similar number will have died in the period after 1990 (Archer 1990). A 2000 study of Navajo miners reported that there were 94 lung-cancer deaths documented among Navajos from 1969–1993, that 63 of these were former uranium miners, and that uranium miners had a risk of 28.6

relative to controls (Gilliland et al. 2000). Frank Gilliland et al. point out that this appears to be a "unique example of exposure in a single occupation accounting for the majority of lung cancers in an entire population" (Gilliland et al. 2000, 278).

The Final Push to Pass RECA

In the 1980s, Perry Charley, who had testified with his father in Utah, and Phil Harrison—both of whom were children whose fathers died following illness due to work in the mines—carried on organizing Navajo people. Charley assisted Udall with *Begay v. US* before helping start the Red Mesa/Mexican Water Four Corners Uranium Committee in 1985. Harrison was elected president of the Uranium Radiation Victims Committee, based in Red Valley and Cove, Arizona, in 1982 (Boden 2000). Organizing, combined with the status of the Navajo people as a sovereign nation, provided the foundation for the effort to pass RECA. It was finally passed in 1990 (Eichstaedt 1994). Some 10,000 workers were employed in uranium mining, and about a quarter of them were Navajo. As of mid-2005, 3,415 uranium miners, 550 millers, and 112 ore transporters had been compensated a total of $407 million.

Conclusions

This history shows a deliberate avoidance by the federal government with respect to the health disaster among uranium miners, even though uranium mining was considered very much a federal matter. Necessary actions were delayed up to two decades beyond when there was ample knowledge to justify a protective stance. And the position of scientists in the government who had the knowledge and often argued for protection was seriously compromised. We are hardly the first to conclude that these delays represent a gross violation of the rights of the miners (Eichstaedt 1994; ACHRE 1995; Moure-Eraso 1999; Brugge et al. 1997; Dawson 1992). Federal regulations for ventilation came nearly 20 years after the need was clear, and only when many miners were sick and dying. Worker-protection revisions proposed by NIOSH have still not been implemented. Earlier efforts to educate mine owners and state officials, and to notify miners, were half-hearted at best. Compensation for those who were sick or died only came after another 20 years, after hundreds had died. And even when compensation was belatedly provided, it was given in a grudging and capricious fashion. The Navajo people suffered along with white and Hispanic miners from these failures. In addition, they were even more poorly informed, and hampered from protecting themselves. And their position with respect to the rules and implementation of the RECA was worse, as we shall see in subsequent chapters.

The one bright spot in this history is the view it affords of communities and labor organizations that identified problems, organized themselves to learn about them, and formed alliances to address them. In the future, government bureaucracies and scientific communities should listen to the representatives of these constituencies and respond appropriately, and in a timely fashion.

Notes

1.   http://www.usdoj.gov/civil/omp/omi/Tre_SysClaimsToDate Sum.pdf (accessed June 17, 2005).

References

Advisory Committee on Human Radiation Experiments (ACHRE). 1995. *Final Report.* Washington, DC: U.S. Government Printing Office.

Archer, V. E. 1990. Testimony before the Committee on Labor and Human Resources, U.S. Senate. February 8.

Archer V. E., H. J. Magnuson, D. A. Holaday, and P. A. Lawrence. 1962. Hazards to health in uranium mining and milling. *Journal of Occupational Medicine* 4:55–60.

Arnstein, A. 1913. Über den sogenannten "Schneeberger Lungenkrebs." *Verhandl. d. Deutsch, Pathol. Gesellschaft* 16:332–42.

Bale, W. F. 1980. Memorandum to the files, March 14, 1951: Hazards associated with radon and thoron. *Health Physics* 38:1062–66.

Ball, H. 1993. *Cancer factories: America's tragic quest for uranium self-sufficiency*. Westport, CT, and London: Greenwood Press.

Begay v. United States, 591 F. Supp. 991, 1007. (Undated)

Behounek, F. 1970. History of the exposure of miners to radon. *Health Physics* 19:56–57.

Boden, L. 2000. Workers' compensation. In Levy and Wegman, eds., *Occupational health: Recognizing and preventing work-related disease and injury*, 4th ed., 237–56. Boston, MA: Lippincott, Williams & Wilkens.

Brugge, D. M., T. Benally, P. Harrison, M. Austin-Garrison, L. Fasthorse-Begay. 1997. *Memories come to us in the rain and the wind: Oral histories and photographs of Navajo uranium miners and their families*. Boston, MA: Tufts School of Medicine.

Brugge, D., T. Benally, P. Harrison, M. Austin-Garrison, C. Stilwell, M. Elsner, K. Bomboy, H. Johnson, L. Fasthorse-Begay. 1999. The Navajo Uranium Miner Oral History and Photography Project. In J. Piper, ed., *Dine Baa Hane Bi Naaltsoos: Collected papers from the seventh through the tenth Navajo Studies Conferences*, 85–96. Window Rock, AZ: Navajo Nation Historic Preservation Department.

Brugge, D., T. Benally. 1998. Navajo Indian voices and faces testify to the legacy of uranium mining. *Cultural Survival Quarterly* 22:16–19.

Brugge, D., T. Benally, E. Yazzie. 1999. Into the nuclear age as a hand mucker: Interview with Navajo George Tutt, former uranium miner. *New Solutions* 9:195–206.

Bullard, R. D., ed. 1994. *Unequal protection: Environmental justice and communities of color*. San Francisco, CA: Sierra Club Books.

Cherniack, M. 1986. *The hawk's nest incident: America's worst industrial disaster*. New Haven and London: Yale University Press.

Committee on the Biological Effects of Ionizing Radiation. 1988. *Health risks of radon and other internally deposited alpha-emitters (BEIR IV)*. Washington, DC: National Academy Press.

———. 1999. *Health effects of exposure to radon (BEIR VI)*. Washington, DC: National Academy Press.

Dawson, S. 1992. Navajo uranium workers and the effects of occupational illness: A case study. *Human Organization* 51:389–97.

Dawson, S. E., P. H. Charley, P. Harrison. 1997. Advocacy and social action among Navajo uranium workers and their families. In Toba Schwaber Kerson and Associates, eds. *Social work in health settings: Practice in context*, 2nd ed., 391–407. New York and London: Haworth Press.

Donaldson, A. W. 1969. The epidemiology of lung cancer among uranium miners. *Health Physics* 16:563–69.

Eichstaedt, P. H. 1994. *If you poison us: Uranium and Native*

Americans. Santa Fe, NM: Red Crane Books.

Gilliland, F. D., W. C. Hunt, M. Pardilla, C. R. Key. 2000. Uranium mining and lung cancer among Navajo men in New Mexico and Arizona, 1969 to 1993. *Journal of Occupational and Environmental Medicine* 42:278–83.

Harley, J. H. 1952. *Sampling and measurement of airborne daughter products of radon.* Ph.D. diss., Rensselaer Polytechnic Institute.

Harley, J. H. 1953. Sampling and measurement of airborne daughter products of radon. *Nucleonics* 11:12–15. (Reprinted in *Health Physics* 38 [1980]: 1067.)

Härting, F. H., and W. Hesse. n.d. Der Lungenkrebs, die Bergkrankheit in den Schneeberger Gruben. *Vierteljahrsschrift fürgerichtliche Medicin und öffentiliches Sanitätswesen* 30:296–308, and 31:102–29, 313–37.

Holaday, D. A. 1969. History of the exposure of miners to radon. *Health Physics* 16:547–52.

Holaday, D. A., D. E. Rushing, P. F. Woolrich, H. L. Kusnetz, W. F. Bale. 1957. *Control of radon and daughters in uranium mines and calculations on biological effects.* PHS publication 494. Washington, DC: U.S. Public Health Service.

Hueper, W. C. 1942. *Occupational tumors and allied diseases.* Springfield, IL: Charles C. Thomas.

Institute of Medicine. 1999. *Toward environmental justice: Research, education, and health policy needs.* Washington, DC: National Academy Press.

Jorgensen, J. G., R. O. Clemmer, R. L. Little, N. J. Owens, L. A. Robbins. n.d. *Native Americans and energy development.* Cambridge, MA: Anthropology Resource Center.

Lorenz, E. 1944. Radioactivity and lung cancer: A critical review of lung cancer in the miners of Schneeberg and Joachimsthal. *Journal of the National Cancer Institute* 5:1–15.

Lundin F. E., J. K. Wagoner, V. E. Archer. 1971. *Radon daughter exposure and respiratory cancer quantitative and temporal aspects.* NIOSH-NIEHS joint monograph no. 1. Washington, DC: U.S. Department of Health, Education, and Welfare.

Mazzocchi and Wodk. 1977. Testimony before the U.S. Senate on the Federal Mine Safety and Health Act of 1977. March 31.

Mendlein, J. M., D. S. Freedman, D. G. Peter, B. Allen, C. A. Percy, C. Ballew, A. H. Mokdad, L. L. White. 1997. Risk factors for coronary heart disease among Navajo Indians: Findings from the Navajo Health and Nutrition Survey. *J. Nutrition*: S2099–S2105.

Moure-Eraso, R. 1999. Observational studies as human experimentation: The uranium mining experience in the Navajo Nation (1947–66). *New Solutions* 9:193–78.

National Institute of Occupational Safety and Health (NIOSH). 1987. *Criteria for a recommended standard for occupational exposure to radon progeny in underground mines.* DHHS [NIOSH] publication no. 88–101. Washington, DC: National Institute of Occupational Safety and Health.

New Mexico Energy Institute. 1976. *Uranium industry in New Mexico.* Albuquerque: Public Finance Research Program, University of New Mexico Energy Resources Board (report no. 76–100B).

Parascandola, M. 2001. Cigarettes and the U.S. Public Health Service in the 1950s. *American Journal of Public Health (AJPH)* 91:196–204.

Pearson, J. 1980. Hazard visibility and occupational health problem solving: The case of the uranium industry. *Journal of Community Health* 6:136–47.

Peller, S. 1939. Lung cancer among mine workers in Joachimsthal. *Human Biology* 11:130–43.

Radiation Exposure Compensation Act of 1981. Hearing before the Senate Committee on Labor and Human Resources, 97th Congress, 1st session (Washington, DC: October 27, 1981).

Radiation Exposure Compensation Act of 1981–Part 2. Hearing before the Senate Committee on Labor and Human Resources, 97th Congress, 2nd session (Salt Lake City, UT: April 8, 1982).

Ringholtz, R. C. 1989. *Uranium frenzy: Boom and bust on the Colorado Plateau.* New York: W. W. Norton & Co.

Roscoe, R. J. 1997. An update of mortality from all causes among white uranium miners from the Colorado Plateau Study Group. *American Journal of Industrial Medicine* 31:211–22.

Roscoe, R. J., J. A. Deddens, A. Salvan, T. M. Schnorr. 1995. Mortality among Navajo uranium miners. *AJPH* 85:535–40.

Rosner, D., and G. Markowitz. 1991. *Deadly dust: Silicosis and the politics of occupational disease in twentieth-century America.* Princeton, NJ: Princeton University Press.

Rothman, D. J. 1991. *Strangers at the bedside: A history of how law and bioethics transformed medical decision making.* New York: Basic Books.

Samet, J. M., D. M. Kurtvirt, R. J. Waxweiler, C. R. Key. 1984. Uranium mining and lung cancer in Navajo men. *N Engl J Med* 310:1481–84.

Samet, J. M., C. L. Wiggins, C. R. Key, T. M. Becker. 1988. Morbidity from lung cancer and chronic obstructive pulmonary disease in New Mexico, 1958–82. *AJPH* 78:1182–86.

Schwartz, R. M. *The legal rights of union stewards.* 1988. Boston, MA: Work Rights Press.

Sievers, M. L. 1968. Cigarette and alcohol usage by southwestern American Indians. *AJPH* 58:71–82.

Smith, B. E. 1987. *Digging our own graves: Coal miners and the struggle over black lung disease.* Philadelphia, PA: Temple University Press.

Stern, J. 1992. *Archival and ethnographic investigations relating to ten Priority II and eight Priority III project areas associated with the Navajo Abandoned Mine Lands Reclamation Department's Sweetwater Program Area.* Window Rock, AZ: Navajo Abandoned Mine Lands Reclamation Department (NNAD 92–021). September.

Tennert, R. A., and M. Litchford. 1998. *White man's medicine: Government doctors and the Navajo, 1863–1955.* Albuquerque: University of New Mexico Press.

Udall, S. L. 1994. *The myths of August: A personal exploration of our tragic cold war affair with the atom.* New York: Pantheon Books.

U.S. Department of Energy (USDOE). 1984. *United States mining and milling industry: A comprehensive review.* A report to the Congress from the President of the United States. May.

U.S. Department of Health, Education and Welfare (USDOH). 1964. *Report of the Advisory Committee to the Surgeon General of the Public Health Service: Smoking and Health.* PHS publication no. 1103. Washington, DC: U.S. GPO.

Woolf, J. 2000. Bill may finally compensate sick Navajo uranium workers. *Salt Lake Tribune,* [n.d.], A1.

Zubeck, P. 1998. Jurors rule against mill: Company ordered to pay $2.9 million. *Colorado Springs Gazette,* July 17, 1–4.

Chapter Four

"HUMAN BEINGS ARE PRICELESS"

INTERVIEW WITH LEROY AND LORRAINE JACK

Interview in Navajo by Phil Harrison, December 1995
Translation/transcription by Esther Yazzie-Lewis
and Timothy Benally

The interview that follows is with Leroy Jack Sr. and Lorraine Jack. They reside 12 miles from Shiprock, in a place called *Gad Ii'ahi*. Mr. Jack was born and raised north of *Bitl'aabito'*. Mrs. Jack was born and raised near Shiprock. They have lived together for about 32 years.

HARRISON: *Okay. Now the questions I will be asking will deal with uranium. When you worked with uranium, when did you first go to work with uranium?*

LEROY JACK: I first went to work for them in 1956 up to 1990. I worked up to that time.

HARRISON: *Why did you go to work with uranium?*

LEROY JACK: I had relatives who worked there, and I went over there and I started working.

HARRISON: *When your spouse went to work there, what did you do?*

Fig. 4.1 Leroy and Lorraine Jack, Cudei, NM, 1995. Photographed by Doug Brugge, courtesy of the Navajo Nation Museum, Window Rock, AZ, Catalog #URC-021.C.

LORRAINE JACK: We would live there where he worked. We lived together as husband and wife. Pretty soon we had children. Our children became young adults and he left the job. I grew up with uranium, because my father works with uranium.

HARRISON: *Who did you work for?*

LEROY JACK: The first mine was Berwell Mining Company who I worked for. I worked for about 10 years for them.

HARRISON: *What was your work when you worked there?*

LEROY JACK: Back then there was not a lot of equipment. They worked with shovels and carts they pushed around. The carts were taken outside and the ore was dumped.

HARRISON: *How were the working conditions when you worked down in the mine?*

LEROY JACK: Back then, there was no ventilation, there was no air. There were fans up on top of the mine and they blew very little air. In my later years of work, they had big holes called bore holes and they blew out a lot of air. The ventilation was strong, but in the earlier years they were very weak.

HARRISON: *Did they have safety equipment for individuals back then?*

LEROY JACK: In some places it was like that. They had respirators and earplugs. And with the clothes, they did not want you to wear ragged clothing. That was a restriction. In some places it is not like that, but in the small mines they did not have ventilation. The bigger mines they took caution for safety and they would have meetings on a regular basis.

HARRISON: *When you worked in the mines, were you ever affected by it?*

LEROY JACK: I did not notice back then, but today I hurt some. Back then it was not like that. The noise from the machines affected my ears. I cannot hear with one ear. Also, my leg, I fell and I broke the skinny bone in my leg.

HARRISON: *Were you compensated for the broken bone?*

LEROY JACK: No.

HARRISON: *I just asked a question about the effects of uranium. Are you affected by it that you know of, or you suspect it could be? Also, your children were born and raised there, you said. How were they affected?*

LORRAINE JACK: Well, just by observing him, he would say he is hurting. He sometimes moans at night—"My arms hurt"—different places, including his legs. He just said that, and then I suddenly would feel pain, too. My left arm was in pain, perhaps it's from working too hard. I just thought at the joint, it felt like when I tried to bend it backward, it really hurt—it just got worse. Then I began to think, "Without a doubt, what he is affected with is affecting me now." It goes all way up to my shoulders and it hurts. Sometimes for no reason, I get pain in my chest. Anyway, I try not to think about it.

Our children were born [near the mines]. As a pregnant mother I used to go there. So, the babies were born there. When they grew up they played there, just as I did. They played in the ore that was dangerous, just as we did way back. I did not know it was dangerous. So, we exposed [our children] all of them to uranium, just as we were exposed to it before. My brothers and sisters were exposed to it; now we did this to our children, I think. So, one of our children who was eight years old, perhaps nine, that one was hospitalized. They told us his heart or lungs were not very strong. So, for that reason, he is under doctor's care and gets a shot every month from the pediatrician. The other one is our first born, who is now 22 or 23 years old. Back then when he was in junior high, he used to say he had pain in the chest. He was told his heart was not very strong also. For that reason he did not join the military service. He sees some boys go there and his desire was to join up, but because of his condition the military services could not accept him, so he never went. Now he just works.

Thinking back now, I wonder if it was from [uranium]. Toward the end we came back and left him there working. He [Mr. Jack] brought back his work clothes when he came back from work, and we washed his clothes in our washing machine. His clothes were caked with mud. When you're over there, you're not aware of the smell, but over here it smelled. Sometimes you had to wash it twice to get them clean.

Harrison: *This uranium was dug out for white people and some for Navajo people—that was what was done, back then. So, these people who ran the mines [contractors] and the mines that were on Navajo land, what do you think of that?*

Leroy Jack: Well, when the mining was in operation, we were not concerned. At this time, many men were harmed—that's what I think about this—so I realized it is dangerous. So, when you talk to those who worked, this is what they say: "We mined dangerous stuff, we didn't know!" It is not good.

Harrison: *How about you? How do you feel about the mines?*

Lorraine Jack: One area of concern, for example, when you purchase a prescription, there is a warning on the drugs. Warning to keep it out of reach of children and to hide it— they make this clear on the prescription. What if in the beginning [employers/government] had kept the men at work and they had not allowed the children to come near the mine sites? The men were sacrificed already, it seems; they already knew, perhaps—they just watched us expose ourselves. It should have been like that from the beginning, I think. They should have told us, "No." At that time they should have provided washing machines so the miners could wash their clothes. Instead, it was like herding sheep into a field of stickers.

HARRISON: *Then from Washington they said they would take care of us in the contracts about 200 years ago, I think it was. They said it in the treaty, and because of it they would take care of us; this is what Washington said to us. So, with that said, do you think the miners were cared for? What do you both think of that?*

LEROY JACK: They did not care for us, because there were areas where the conditions were not good. There were no ventilators. That is not looking out for the well-being of people.

LORRAINE JACK: I have spoken on this before. Right from the beginning they should have told the families to live away from the mine site. The mines were right there; that is the way the families lived. It was a dangerous substance and they did not take care of us. Children were exposed to it, and it contaminated our food and our drinking water. They should have said, "Do not drink the water in the mine, but here is drinking water." A lot of times there was no water over there. It would have been good if they had good water available for the employees. In the summer time when it was hot, the mine workers would go down into the mine to get water because there was cold water down there. They drank that water; they did not know it was bad water.

HARRISON: *There is compensation, and some people barely are getting paid. What do you think of this?*

LEROY JACK: It should not be difficult for them to be paid. It has been several years. They turned me down, and finally I was compensated. It should not be a difficult process, and they should not give the people a hard time. It would be good this way. Their physical conditions have been affected, and some have died off. There were many men I worked with who have died, and some are experiencing health problems. That is why, even though you are not affected now, in time it will affect you. So, they should not give people a hard time in compensating them.

HARRISON: *How about you?*

LORRAINE JACK: He spoke of it well. There are some who really want to be compensated, and they go to the hospital for it. They pawn their things to have gas money to get to the hospital, and they would like to use this money to get their pawns out. They hope for this, and they [the government] seem to be giving them a difficult time and it is not good. They tell them, "This is how much you will be paid," and they give the people anticipation of money to be paid, and they want x-rays. People are reaching out to receive the money, but they cannot reach it. It is almost like someone has money in their hands and the people are chasing around after them. They are trying to reach for the money, and in the process, they are stumbling and hurting themselves while they are chasing after the money. There are some who are very unhealthy and they can't really enjoy it. They are not interested.

His father is like that. That is why I think this. What if he had been compensated when he was still healthy and worked with the tractor? He would have been able to enjoy it. Now, he can't enjoy it. Now he is in a wheelchair. We have all been exposed to uranium, and then the gratitude of the one hundred thousand dollars is just not enough. The people have been contaminated, it is in their blood, and some children never got to see their fathers come home to them. Money is something that just disappears in your hands, and human beings are priceless. Human beings can greet you all their life. Money does not greet you. Your father, husband, brother can greet you. For us, there are many relatives who did not come back to their families. They went into the mines and never came back out. Some have come back out, but they have health problems. A lot of them to this day are pleading to be paid.

HARRISON: *In the future, if they say that there is still uranium to be mined and they want to mine it—what do you think of that?*

LEROY JACK: What I think is that it is dangerous. We have leaders—what do they think of it? For me, it has affected and hurt many of my relatives; that is why I do not like it.

LORRAINE JACK: They should say, "No," and there are many people who know about it. Why should it be? Because uranium is dangerous. Why would you run into the fire when it is hot?—it is like that. The people know this. For myself, I think it is dangerous. Whoever wants it, I am sure they have it in their land; let them dig it out there.

HARRISON: *There are uranium mines, mills, and waste piled up and left abandoned—what do you think of this?*

LEROY JACK: It would be good to clean it up. I used to work in Colorado, and they said they wanted to shut down the mine. We put everything back into the mine and we covered it back up. There was nothing left on top, and it was replanted with grass. The same thing is happening there in Slick Rock, now. They are putting everything back into the mine and covering it up with new soil on top. It would be good this way, to hide it.

HARRISON: *From here into the future, about five, ten, 50, 100, 200 years, there will be several generations of grandchildren. What should be taught to them? This is this way . . . uranium is this. How will the words be put to them?*

LEROY JACK: They already know from what is being said now. My children are like that. They are told this is what uranium does, and they know. They know uranium is not good. That is how they think. I say that, and if I did not work with uranium maybe I would not be this way. My physical being would be good, is what I tell my children.

LORRAINE JACK: There are two older children who really are aware of uranium. Your father is like this, his x-rays are like this, and his health is like this, I say to them. They say, "Why couldn't he have worked somewhere else? We are all exposed." They then say, "There was a treaty and an agreement was made, is what we learned at school; but this is not respected today." They have become men. And when the others become men, then they would think of it then. And we tell the children that uranium work is not good and they should get a good job.

HARRISON: *We are almost done, just a couple more things. We have asked questions about uranium and you talked about your experience. Is there something you would like to say that you have not mentioned? Is there a concern you have?*

LEROY JACK: The homes were next to the mine. It is said that the families should have been told not to live too close to the mine. That is true. When there was blasting done down in the mine, the smoke would come out of the mine and blow toward the homes. It is true; no one should have been around in that area, I think.

HARRISON: *How about you?*

LORRAINE JACK: You could clearly see the smoke come out of the mine and the children would be running through it. This is a big concern to me. He wanted to work, and they should have told us he was the only one allowed there at the work site and the families are not allowed, is what they should have said. Instead we were all exposed to it. This I do not like. They just watched us. They did not go to schools to educate about the effects of uranium. They might have said, "Uranium is this way." One could say I should have said this. I had a chance to say this and I should have said this, they say. Then there are others who are afraid to say anything because they think it may be used against them in the future. Because of that, they are afraid to say anything. We Navajo people are very respectful. This is a big hindrance for us.

Chapter Five

ADVOCACY AND SOCIAL ACTION AMONG NAVAJO PEOPLE

URANIUM WORKERS AND THEIR FAMILIES, 1988–1995

Susan E. Dawson, Perry H. Charley,
and Phillip Harrison Jr.[*]

Personal Involvement in the Issue

As a researcher from Utah State University, Susan went to the Navajo Nation in the summer of 1988 to interview uranium miners and their families about the psychosocial effects of not being compensated for occupational illnesses. Susan and a colleague, Gary E. Madsen, returned in 1992 to interview uranium mill workers. [Milling of uranium is the second stage of the nuclear fuel cycle, following the mining of uranium ore, in which the ore is crushed, leached, and refined into uranium oxides or yellowcake.] During these studies, Susan met Perry Charley and Phil Harrison, both Navajo people, who were longtime activists associated with uranium issues. Their fathers had worked in the uranium mines, and Phil had worked as a uranium miner for a

---

* This article was originally published as "Advocacy and social action among Navajo uranium workers and their families," in Toba Schwaber Kerson and Associates, eds., *Social work in health settings: Practice in context*, 2nd ed., 391–407 (New York and London: Haworth Press, 1997).

summer during high school. When their fathers, Harris Charley and Phillip Harrison Sr., died with illnesses associated with uranium mining, Perry and Phil worked actively to redress the uranium miners' plight.

This chapter focuses on Perry and Phil's advocacy and social action on behalf of the uranium miners, mill workers, and their families. Susan's role as a social-work academic involved conducting the two studies of interviews with uranium miners, mill workers, and their families; presenting information at public and professional meetings; publishing the studies' results in scholarly journals and book chapters; and testifying at congressional hearings on behalf of the uranium workers.

Policy

Beginning in the 1960s, illnesses among the Navajo uranium miners became evident, with workers becoming critically ill and dying. The ten-year-or-longer latency period was taking its toll on workers and their families. A series of lawsuits on behalf of nuclear-test downwind victims and underground uranium miners were tried, and failed due to the discretionary-function exception of the Federal Tort Claims Act (FTCA). Following the lawsuits, Senator Ted Kennedy (D-Massachusetts) introduced four compensation bills in 1979. Other bills were introduced by Senator Orrin Hatch (R-Utah) in 1981 and 1983, and later by Hatch and Congressman Wayne Owens (D-Utah) in 1989. Finally in 1990, the Hatch-Owens bill, the Radiation Exposure Compensation Act (RECA), provided compassionate payment to underground uranium miners, civilian downwinders of the atomic testing program, and eventually nuclear-test-site workers.

Prior to RECA, the only state to compensate uranium-miner claims was Colorado. Only those workers who could establish a work record in that state were eligible to apply for and receive benefits. Consequently until 1990, Navajo uranium miners were for the most part ineligible for compensation and suffered greatly, economically and emotionally (Dawson 1992).

Compensation under 1990 RECA allowed for a payment of $100,000, $75,000, and $50,000 for underground uranium miners, nuclear-test-site workers, and downwind atomic victims respectively, and was paid from a $100 million trust fund administered by the U. S. Department of Justice (DOJ). If the claimant was deceased, the payment was made to the widow/widower and/or survivor.

For the uranium miners, the worker or survivor could apply if he had worked in a mine located in Arizona, Colorado, New Mexico, Utah, or Wyoming between January 1, 1947, and December 31, 1971. Working Level Months (WLM) of exposure to radiation were established in which a nonsmoker needed 200 WLM. A smoker who developed a specific, listed respiratory disease or cancer before the age of 45 needed 300 WLM, while a smoker who developed a listed disease after the age of 45 needed 500 WLM. The diseases included any type of lung cancer, fibrosis of the lung, pulmonary fibrosis, cor pulmonale related to fibrosis of the lung—or, if the miner worked in a uranium mine within an Indian reservation, moderate or severe silicosis, or moderate or severe pneumoconiosis. Workers and their survivors could file claims up to 20 years after 1990 (Office of Navajo Uranium Workers, n.d.).

Technology and Organizations

There are several organizations that offer services and support to uranium workers and their families, including the Indian Health Service (IHS) hospitals, the Office of Navajo Uranium Workers, and four uranium-worker support groups.

The PHS operates the Indian Health Service hospitals on the Navajo Nation. These hospitals provide health care free of charge to the Navajo people and are generally staffed with family practitioners, internists, and pediatricians. Many of the physicians work at the IHS for a few years and then move off the reservation to private practices. One of the common complaints heard by patients is that they do not have a family doctor who stays long enough to know the family and their medical history. Moreover, the IHS system does not employ pulmonary specialists as a rule. These specialists are needed to fully diagnose respiratory problems. In attempting to document their cases, miners needed to have health examinations that included chest x-rays.

In the past, the Navajo Nation brought in their own pulmonary specialist, Dr. Leon S. Gottlieb, who was the first physician to associate and document lung cancer and uranium mining among the Navajo people (Gottlieb and Husen 1982). When uranium miners were identified as possibly having lung cancer or nonmalignant respiratory disease, the miner was referred off the reservation to specialists and hospitals in such places as Albuquerque and Denver. These hospital visits were paid for by the IHS system, including travel to and from the facility; however, lodging and food were not paid for the family member(s) accompanying the patient. This often created a hardship for families because of the expense. Widows and family members related to Susan that they would often spend the night in a chair with the miner because they could not afford to stay in a motel. They would also bring their own food or go without. Phil explains:

> My Dad wasn't quite sure if he was going to make it through Christmas and through New Year's, and we had the hardest time there going back and forth to the hospital [about a four-hour drive]. . . . We took him in and out for radiation treatment in Albuquerque. We'd leave him there for about two weeks at a time, go pick him up, and bring him back. And it was a lot of work doing that. My other brothers and sisters were still in school. They were small. So finally he passed away in January of 1971 from lung cancer, and from there on it was a lot of responsibility left up to me to take care of my Mom and the family.

For the most part, physicians did not speak Navajo, and it was common for patients to not understand their diagnoses and treatment plans. Susan and Gary often heard the miners/millers explain that they had "red lungs" or "uranium on the lungs" in place of the diagnosis of nonmalignant respiratory

Fig. 5.1 Phil Harrison, Mitten Rock, AZ, 1995. Photographed by Doug Brugge, courtesy of the Navajo Nation Museum, Window Rock, AZ, Catalog #URC-020.C.

disease. Also, if the treating professional did not understand the Navajo culture, they might not realize that the patient could believe that a natural event, such as lightning, might be considered responsible for the patient's illness, rather than an occupational exposure. A result of the latter would be that the patient and family would not pursue compensation or work-related benefits.

According to Perry and Phil, a comprehensive health-care system separate from the IHS, with a uranium clinic designed for miners and other uranium workers who are ill, is needed. Phil noted that miners with lung cancer are often too sick to travel off the reservation or to wait in IHS waiting rooms for long periods until they are called. When he visited Japan in 1991 as part of a delegation of American Indians concerned with uranium issues, he toured such a government-funded hospital for the Hibakusha, the bombing victims of Hiroshima and

Nagasaki. He said that the hospital, in addition to treating the Hibakusha, also conducts studies of their own on the effects of radiation exposure. In recent years, a pulmonary clinic was established at Northern Navajo Medical Center, largely addressing this concern.

The IHS has contracted recently with the University of New Mexico School of Medicine and the Miners' Colfax Medical Center in Raton, New Mexico, to operate a screening van. Miners can receive x-rays and testing free of charge through this service. Also, the IHS took x-rays of uranium workers and sent them to be read by B-readers[1] off the reservation.

The Office of Navajo Uranium Workers, which is a central registry for uranium miners and mill workers funded by the Navajo Nation, grew out of a grass-roots movement that began in the Red Valley and Cove, Arizona, area of the reservation. Perry's involvement began in 1975 when he noticed that his father began having increasing difficulties with his breathing:

> I was aware that [my father] had spent over twenty
> years in the underground mines on the Navajo Indian
> Reservation and the Colorado Plateau. I started mak-
> ing the connections that his previous employment in
> these mines may have caused his respiratory prob-
> lems. This prompted me to find out what had actually
> happened to him. I found out quickly that his was not
> the only case, that there were countless others with
> similar disabling and progressive health problems.

Perry worked throughout the 1970s and 1980s in various projects to educate the Navajo people about radiation. After 1975 he was employed as a supervisor for the Community Health Representative (CHR) Program, a grass-roots health-advocacy program with the Tribe. He initiated and revised the program's goals and objectives to emphasize increased public awareness through direct coordination with the Shiprock IHS medical staff, and through an intensive educational network with the affected communities. Information was disseminated at chapter-house meetings, group presentations, schools, and annual fairs/events, using television networks, radios, and one-on-one contacts with family members in homes. (Chapter houses are units of Navajo Nation government established for different community areas.)

In 1978 Perry worked with Dr. Lora M. Shields, a visiting biology professor at the Shiprock Navajo Community College, on a 12-year March of Dimes Birth Defect Study. He also worked with Stewart L. Udall on the attorney's lawsuits—including *Begay v. United States of America*, on behalf of the Navajo uranium miners—and worked with him as claims were processed by DOJ for compassionate payment under RECA. Beginning in 1978, he gathered mining histories for uranium miners and their surviving families and forwarded the information to Udall's Phoenix office. Perry states:

> Initially, meetings were held at chapter houses for clients. These were much easier than traveling from home to home, though this had to be performed on some difficult cases when necessary. We also had to establish a special office under the Shiprock CHR Program for the specific purpose of obtaining information for Udall's lawsuit when more and more Navajos from all parts of the Navajo Nation started getting involved. This was, in essence, the first Navajo Uranium Office.

Phil noted that when he and others would meet with legislators, tribal officials, or go to conferences, people would ask about the statistics of the uranium workers to justify requests for funding and/or compensation. Trips were made to Washington, DC, and during the tribal leadership of Leonard Haskie and Ervin Billy, the Office of Navajo Uranium Workers was established in April 1990 in Red Valley, Arizona.

Four support groups—two for the uranium miners and two for the uranium mill workers—have evolved over the past 20 years. Red Valley's Uranium Radiation Victims Committee was organized in the early 1970s to provide support and technical assistance to uranium miners and their families. In 1978 they invited the CBS television network to document the continued plight of uranium miners.

It was during this visit that a staff member of the Navajo Environmental Protection Commission, using a gamma scintillation counter, noticed that a uranium worker's home was "hot" with radioactivity. Eventually, 17 homes in the Oak Springs, Arizona, area were discovered to have been built with radioactive tailings (dirt and rocks) left over from uranium mining. Perry was part of a committee that was formed in the Shiprock area specifically for the purpose of identifying any additional habitable structures containing low-level radioactivity. They also prioritized these homes for remediation, locating and acquiring federal monies to replace them and coordinating with tribal and federal agencies in their radiological surveys. Such homes were eventually replaced or renovated to acceptable housing standards. Despite these efforts, Navajo Nation officials were unwilling to assist by obligating tribal monies for replacement homes.

The Red Valley support group elected Phil as their chairman in 1982. The group met monthly and worked on organizing around the uranium legislation, health issues, the uranium registry, cleanup of homes, and reclamation of uranium mines and mills. Initially there were not that many people who attended the meetings; however, over time the meetings grew to include as many as 100 people. Announcements on the radio and in newspapers were made to advertise the meetings. The Red Valley Committee was instrumental in voicing concerns of the uranium miners and their surviving families to the Navajo government. They also contacted congressional delegates at the federal level in attempts to enact legislation to compensate the workers and their families. At first, Navajo Nation officials were not interested, but this slowly changed over time as the national and international news media continued documenting the problems the uranium workers were encountering.

Perry assisted in starting the Red Mesa/Mexican Water Four Corners Uranium Committee in 1985. This support group had similar intentions to the Red Valley Committee. Their goals and objectives were to disseminate information nationally about the plight of the Navajo uranium miners. The committee was further assisted by an elected chairman, who happened to have ties to the Associated Press (AP) through his work with a local TV station. He later went on to become the community's Council delegate. The committee was in existence until the enactment of 1990 RECA.

Prior to RECA's enactment, Phil and Perry would update the people at chapter-house meetings. At one Mexican Water chapter meeting, over 300 people attended to hear the status of the bill and its meaning for them individually. These types of meetings were held throughout the Navajo Nation to apprise people of RECA and to network with each other.

Because the uranium-mill workers were excluded from 1990 RECA due to a lack of conclusive studies, two support groups were formed among the millers. A Navajo miller approached Phil and asked him if he was interested in developing a millers' group. Organized in Shiprock, New Mexico, in 1992, the Four Corners Uranium Millers Association met monthly and included about 100 members. Initially, the group set out to collect data on the millers. They cooperated with Susan and Gary by participating in their study with the mill workers. The other mill-workers' group, the Western Navajo Agency Millers at Tonalea, Arizona, is located on the western portion of the Navajo Nation, while Shiprock is on the eastern side.

Practice in Context
Definition of the Client

Within this context, the client is the group of uranium miners, mill workers, and their families. As of August 1995, the Office of Navajo Uranium Workers had registered 2,449 uranium workers, with 1,700 miners and 400 millers identified. The two groups are not mutually exclusive since 200 of the workers were employed as both miners and millers. Of the miners who have registered, 1,500–1,600 meet the criteria for RECA eligibility (Benally 1995).

By August 1995, 280 uranium miners or their survivors had been compensated. Many of these cases were originally denied, and with the assistance of the Office of Navajo Uranium Workers, their cases were reopened and finally accepted. When a case is denied, the claimant has 60 days to appeal. When claims were denied, it was usually because of inadequate information, such as insufficient WLM or smoking data and/or lack of proof of compensable disease. When compensation started in 1992, DOJ denied claims without documentation of marriage or death certificate. Many elderly Navajo people were married through traditional weddings or lived in common-law arrangements. Death and birth certificates often were unavailable, especially when the worker was born and/or died at home. Mr. Benally, then director of the Office of Navajo Uranium Workers, presented this information to then Navajo Nation President Petersen Zah, and it was arranged in early 1993 that a tribal judge in a tribal court could certify these life events.

In addition to the Office, Navajo miners could file their cases on their own or through attorneys. For those who do file through an attorney, it was stipulated under 1990 RECA that the attorney may receive no more than $10,000 from the claimant's award.

Goals

While the client is identified as a group, it is important to recognize that the goals that are applied to the group are appropriate in context for individuals within the group. The value of self-determination is an important one for the social-work profession (Zastrow 1993), and it is also important within the Navajo value structure. The practice of social work with American Indians suggests a practice of noninterference (Good Tracks 1973). Phil illustrates this principle with regard to a uranium miner who had not applied for RECA, nor registered with the Office of Navajo Uranium Workers:

> I know one person who heard about all the setbacks
> and all the frustrations that all the people are going
> through [with RECA] to where he doesn't even want to
> do anything about it. He hasn't even registered or
> filed—a miner with some twenty years experience.
> And I hate to go there and say, "Hey, look, here's what's
> going on and do you want to file?" I'd be kind of
> imposing on him. And I don't want to do that unless
> somebody asks for help, and then I can help them.

One way to address this issue would be through the dissemination of information and education about radiation exposure and RECA through chapter-house meetings, congressional hearings, the media, and workshops. In this way, workers and their family members would become aware of the information, resources, and options available to them. They might then decide to formulate a plan of action, which might include seeking assistance from others.

Education and dissemination of information about the issues are two important goals for activists working with the uranium workers and their families. Other goals include helping people to register with the Office of Navajo Uranium Workers, to apply for RECA, and to seek technical and emotional support through various support groups, chapter houses, Navajo government, and other institutions and networks. In some instances, it is important to go door-to-door to accomplish sharing of information. Phil explains that interviewing people for another project gave him an opportunity to update them on what was happening with RECA. He notes why going to peoples' homes is important:

> And I would say to this day there's a lot of people
> that have not even filed with the uranium office yet.
> They have not even started filing a claim for compensation. It's because they're way out there on the reservation. Because of their economic situation, and
> there's no transportation. There's no money to pay
> for gas to come out.

Both Perry and Phil, in working with Dr. Shields in the 1980s, went with her to chapter houses every other month to disseminate educational information. These meetings and Dr. Shields's study were announced on the radio since most families listen to the Navajo station around noontime to hear about chapter and community events. Dr. Shields would define radiation and its potential effects on people. Background information about the history of the atomic age was also presented, along with slide shows. Phil believes that this was one of the things that induced people eventually to listen and to attend meetings about RECA.

One other goal, which is a larger environmental community one, is the remediation of abandoned uranium mines and mills. Perry was employed under the Uranium Mill Tailings Remediation and Control Act (UMTRCA) Project from 1982 through 1988 under the U.S. Department of Energy (DOE) to reclaim uranium mill sites located on the Navajo Reservation. In addition to assuring compliance to contract specifications in reclaiming these mill sites, he was responsible in forming citizens' groups at each Navajo UMTRCA site. These groups consisted of local people, so that adequate public input could be obtained throughout the remedial-action process. Part of his duties involved keeping local residents informed about the remediation activities. To explain technical nuclear terms, Perry assisted in developing a video of various UMTRCA activities in the Navajo language.

Perry was then offered employment in Shiprock with the Navajo Abandoned Mine Lands Reclamation (AML) Department in 1988. This is a federally funded tribal department under the U.S. Department of Interior's Office of Surface Mining Control Reclamation and Enforcement. It delegated responsibilities to reclaim mine sites abandoned without adequate reclamation prior to 1977. The AML program established tribal protocol and schemes for the prioritization of abandoned mine sites, and established in-house guidelines for cleanup of radioactively contaminated lands and reclamation of radioactive mine sites. Efforts under AML included taking physical inventory of 1,100 abandoned mine sites located within the boundaries of the Navajo Nation, prioritizing mines according to their degree of physical hazard, and initiating construction activities.

Abandoned mines posed a threat to the Navajo people in that these sites were unreclaimed, unfenced, and accessible. It was not uncommon for children to play in these "caves," and for cattle, sheep, and goats to wander into them for warmth. The sites were as old as 40 to 50 years and unstable. In many of the sites, mine waste could travel into washes or streambeds, posing hazards to people and livestock downstream. Perry illustrates:

> We found approximately 500 mines that were used by
> local shepherds for livestock pens. A well-insulated
> sheep pen, but potentially dangerous to the sheep that
> used the mines for shelter and lambing. One lady told
> me in the Tse-Tah area in northwest Arizona, "I always
> wondered why my lambs were born without fleece and
> why some were born deformed or with limbs missing."
> She lived about 200 feet away from a mine for many
> years, using the mine for a livestock pen. The family
> was in the process of building an addition to their
> home using the radioactive mine waste.

Another pathway for human exposure is through ingesting exposed animals' organs, such as the kidneys, in which radioactive elements are concentrated. Eating the livestock's organs is a common practice among the Navajo people and therefore of considerable concern.

Contract

While there is no written contract per se, there is a sense of obligation to work with this group of uranium workers and their families, and to obtain compensation through the RECA program. The Office of Navajo Uranium Workers assists uranium-mining clients who apply for RECA through the Office. Once the client is registered, the process of obtaining compensation is maintained until compensation is either granted or denied.

Hindsight indicates that what has occurred is not unlike the social-action campaigns of the 1960s civil-rights period. Activists have worked largely on their own, without pay, networking and traveling across the Navajo Nation and to Washington, DC, to promote legislation and the uranium workers' cause. Phil relates:

> Eighty percent of [costs of travel to Washington, DC]
> is out of our own pockets. All during this time. And we
> lost a lot of money over this thing, and I don't think I
> can ever get back the money that I spent on these
> projects. . . . I don't know how long I can stay and put
> up with this thing. My family's really getting after me
> for this. They keep asking me to look for a real job
> that pays. But I said, "One more year."

Meeting Place

In the above discussion, meeting places include workers' homes, support-group meetings, government-agency offices, chapter-house meetings, and congressional offices. In addition to the monthly support-group and committee meetings, chapter meetings were held periodically to update chapter members on RECA information. These were well-attended meetings, numbering in the hundreds at the larger chapters, in which information would be presented, followed by a question-and-answer period.

Other important meeting places included congressional hearings in which activists and uranium workers provided testimonies regarding their plight. All three authors have testified on behalf of the uranium workers. Recent hearings of the President's Advisory Committee on Human Radiation Experimentation included testimonies concerning both the uranium miners and mill workers.

Phil has also traveled internationally on behalf of the uranium workers—to Japan, as previously discussed, and also to Salzburg, Austria, for the World Uranium Hearing (see chapter 1). For the hearings, he and other American Indians presented their stories to "Listeners" about the effects of uranium mining on Indian lands. The Listeners included nuclear experts and other professionals.

Use of Time

As with many social problems, especially in the environmental area, it is grass-roots social action that brings the issue to public awareness. Edelstein (1988, 144) notes, "The development of community organizations tends to provide people with a new sense of power in the midst of a situation that otherwise produces an overall sense of loss of control." The uranium workers and their families have been able to release some of their frustrations and fears through working together with activists, health-care professionals, attorneys, social workers, and legislators. All of these resource people have provided technical assistance and social support to these individuals.

Moreover, people working in social-action campaigns often respond to a multiplicity of events, some of which occur at the same time (Rubin and Rubin 1992). In some campaigns, activists have the luxury of responding in a well-orchestrated fashion, while in others they find themselves reacting by a "seat-of-the-pants" method. In the Navajo uranium-workers' case, there was enough time to organize a grass-roots effort to push compensation forward. Activists were able to work both with individuals and institutions to accomplish their agenda for the most part.

In addition to working with other individuals and bureaucracies, the Navajo people supported each other. Since the Navajo people are clan-based, there is an extended family network that provides social support. Family members ensure that widows and elderly parents are not alone during the difficult period of illness and death. Traditional elders may not have the financial and emotional resources to cope with bureaucracies. In this capacity, older children are able to act as intermediaries between their parents or grandparents and these often complex health, legal, and social systems. Conversely, Perry explains how traditional elders who are ill may act with respect to their families:

To the Navajos, a house that one dies in should never
be used again as the deceased's spirit (*chiidi*) lingers
within. Rather than to condemn a family home, I saw
several miners move out of their comfortable houses
and reside in shacks or arbor shades. Towards the end,
and just before he went into an irreversible coma due
to his complete respiratory failure from which he
never revived, my father did the same thing. "It makes
me breathe better as the house is too confining and
out here I can breathe the fresh clean air," he used to
say. A way of making us feel better? Or was he letting
us, the family, go gradually?

Treatment Modality and Stance of the Social Worker

Advocacy and social action are the treatment modality and
stance of the three authors. A systems approach is also
employed, given the role of linking individuals with various
institutions on and off the reservation. The goal of advocacy
and social action is empowerment of the individual, the group,
and the community. The tragedy that has occurred in the
Navajo Nation with regard to the uranium workers and their
families has left many individuals feeling victimized and
betrayed (Dawson 1992). Perry explains:

> I observed [people's] anguish over events they were
> unknowingly subjected to by an uncaring industry and
> a government whose sole purpose was to procure a
> potentially hazardous and fatal material at all costs.
> Relief in the form of payment for the wrongful injuries
> sustained in the course of their employment and in
> the form of inadequate health care delivery system [is
> slow]. Close to 20 years has passed and I see very little
> difference or improvement.

Linking people to needed resources is important, and yet difficult on the largely rural reservation. Susan interviewed widows
who were eligible for Social Security who had never heard of

the benefit. These same widows, many of whom did not speak English, often did not have telephones, or money for stamps and stationery. In addition, it is unknown how many workers/families across the reservation have not applied for RECA who may be eligible. Consequently, there is great need for assisting people to access the various systems.

In working one-on-one with patients within the IHS, for example, it was beneficial to not only have someone who understood uranium but also someone who was Navajo. Perry was brought in by an IHS physician at the Shiprock Hospital to assist in informing a 50-year-old miner that he had contracted lung cancer, the deadly oat-cell carcinoma. Perry states:

> The physician felt I could relate better with [the miner]
> rather than a nurse or a regular hospital staff person.
> I had to show him his x-rays of his chest, pointing out
> that the dark areas in the photo were cancerous. I
> explained what cancer was. He had very little compre-
> hension of what this meant...I visited him at his
> home in Sweetwater, Arizona, several times until his
> death in the summer of 1980. He told me he didn't
> want to die in "that hospital" but he had to go in...
> He was also distrustful of the Anglos, the hospitals,
> and the government that allowed such a thing to
> happen to him.

In trying to comply with RECA, workers and their families often had to make extra all-day trips, a hardship, to furnish additional employment documents. In cases where no such documents were available, it would help to refresh people's memories by asking where they worked when a particular child was born. Being knowledgeable about events that took place that coincided with their mining history helped also. In certain cases, revisiting the mines in which they had worked and reestablishing their work history were necessary. The stress of dealing with RECA and the overall situation often took its toll on individuals and families. Perry describes the social stress created from the death of a uranium miner on a Navajo family:

> Wives were hit the hardest when a husband contracted the fatal lung disease. The wife had to assume a role they were taught belonged with the male. Many had very little education, no work experience, and consequently ended up on welfare. This was a blow to their ego, their upbringing and [it was] embarrassing. Navajos are taught never to "beg" for handouts to feed and clothe their children. I recall one wife, rather than face these, chose to divorce the miner. A constant battle to feed the family resulted in the oldest children dropping out of school and starting employment or to care for the father. [The father] was a strong central figure; when [he was] no longer available, [it] resulted in family stress, disciplinary/emotional problems, alcoholism among the children [becoming] rampant, and worse.

Use of Outside Resources

The use of outside resources, in this instance resources from off the reservation, have helped to support the work being conducted in the Navajo Nation. Working with universities, law firms, and legislators have proven beneficial. Phil would bring in experts to chapter meetings to explain and educate the people about radiation issues, such as a biology graduate student from the University of New Mexico. Without Perry and Phil's assistance, Susan and Gary would have had great difficulty conducting their work. Perry and Phil provided them with key contacts, information, and support throughout their work, as Perry and Phil did with Stewart Udall, Lora Shields, and others. And in exchange for their outside contact with individuals and government agencies, Perry and Phil received support and help to further their cause.

Case Conclusion

The struggle of the uranium miners, mill workers, and their families will be partially concluded when compensation from

RECA is awarded to the last person who is eligible, and when cleanup of the mine and mill sites is completed. What is difficult to assess, however, is how long it will take for the devastating psychological and social effects to abate. Perry notes that, even when compensation is awarded, "my Dad remains dead and I remain bitter; so continues the legacy of the Navajo uranium miners."

All of the people associated with uranium mining, milling, and environmental contamination have participated in a technological disaster. A technological disaster is human-made as opposed to an act of God, such as a tornado or an earthquake. The effects of long-term chronic disasters are often devastating and lingering, creating fear and anxiety not unlike post-traumatic stress syndrome (Baum 1988; Dawson 1993; Edelstein 1988; Roberts 1993; Vyner 1988). While compensation and remediation are addressed, many questions are left unanswered for the uranium victims. Will I or a family member become ill? Will my unborn children be affected? Is the water safe to drink? Should we move somewhere else? Until stability is brought to the community through long-term efforts, including counseling and traditional healing ceremonies, these questions remain unanswered.

Differential Discussion

It is difficult to determine what could have been done differently in this effort to obtain social justice for the uranium workers and their families. Given the immense resources of the United States government, it is a testament to the Navajo people and activists that justice was served. Overall, it was a successful effort to obtain compassionate payment, and an apology from the government for past wrongdoings.

Practice in Context

Public policy has underscored the lives of the uranium workers and their families since the 1940s. Beginning with the secrecy of the atomic era through the passage of the Radiation Exposure Compensation Act in 1990, the Navajo people have had to react to policies that have threatened the very fabric of their lives. In addition, they have had to respond to large-scale bureaucracies and governmental agencies, which often have not had their best interests in mind. Perry reflects:

> The U.S. government enacted a law (RECA) for "compassionate payment." Many of the uranium miners and their families see little compassion when the very federal agency, the Department of Justice, that had adamantly opposed the establishment of such a law is entrusted to fairly administer the program. These administrators do not have the basic knowledge of the Navajo culture and traditions, and these traditions and values continue to dominate the Navajo way of life.

Reacting to public policies proves constructive when advocacy and social-action approaches are utilized successfully, as in the case of the Navajo uranium workers and their families. Working through both conventional and unconventional methods, a sense of personal and collective control and empowerment was gained.

While this social-action campaign may appear to be enabled by a few activists and leaders, it actually entails the efforts of all the participants, including the uranium workers, their families, and community residents. As is often the case, those most affected by an issue are often most likely to bring it into the public domain. The activists and helping professionals in this instance worked with the participants as resource people. Within this context, practice becomes a powerful tool to effect change and to encourage social justice.

Notes

1.   A "B-reader" has special training in how to read x-rays for non-malignant respiratory disease.

References

Archer, V. E. 1983. Diseases of uranium miners. In W. M. Rom, ed., *Environmental and occupational medicine*, 687–91. Boston: Little, Brown and Company.

Ball, H. 1993. *Cancer factories: America's tragic quest for uranium self-sufficiency.* Westport, CT, and London: Greenwood Press.

Baum, A. 1988. Disasters, natural and otherwise. *Psychology Today* 22 (4): 57–60.

Fleming, R., and L. M. Davidson. 1983. Natural disaster and technological catastrophe. *Environment and Behavior* 15 (3): 333–54.

Fleming, R., and J. E. Singer. 1983. Coping with victimization by technological disaster. *Journal of Social Issues* 39 (2): 117–38.

Benally, T. H. (Director, Office of Navajo Uranium Workers). 1995. Personal communication with Susan Dawson. August 1, 1995.

Dawson, S. E. 1992. Navajo uranium workers and the effects of occupational illnesses: A case study. *Human Organization* 51 (4): 389–97.

Dawson, S. E. 1993. Social work practice and technological disasters: The Navajo uranium experience. *Journal of Sociology and Social Welfare* 20 (2): 5–20.

Edelstein, M. R. 1988. *Contaminated communities: The social and psychological impacts of residential toxic exposure.* Boulder, CO: Westview Press.

Eichstaedt, P. H. 1994. *If you poison us: Uranium and Native Americans.* Santa Fe, NM: Red Crane Books.

Good Tracks, J. G. 1973. Native American noninterference. *Social Work* 18 (6): 30–34.

Gottlieb, L. S., and L. A. Husen. 1982. Lung cancer among Navajo uranium miners. *Chest* 8:449–52.

Office of Navajo Uranium Workers. n.d. Summary of Radiation Exposure Compensation Act. Information sheet.

Roberts, J. T. 1993. Psychosocial effects of workplace hazardous exposures: Theoretical synthesis and preliminary findings. *Social Problems* 40 (1): 74–89.

Rubin, H., and I. Rubin. 1992. *Community organizing and development.* 2nd ed. New York: Maxwell Macmillan International.

Samet, J. M., R. A. Young, M. V. Morgan, C. G. Humble, G. R. Epler, and T. C. McLoud. 1984. Prevalence survey of respiratory abnormalities in New Mexico uranium miners. *Health Physics* 46 (2): 361–70.

Vyner, H. M. 1988. *Invisible trauma: The psychosocial effects of the invisible environmental contaminants.* Lexington, MA: Lexington Books.

Zastrow, C. 1993. *Introduction to social work and social welfare.* 5th ed. Pacific Grove, CA: Brooks/Cole Publishing Company.

Chapter Six

"OUR CHILDREN ARE AFFECTED BY IT"

ORAL HISTORY OF FORMER MINER GEORGE LAPAHIE

Interview in Navajo by Timothy Benally, December 1995
Translation/transcription by Esther Yazzie-Lewis
and Timothy Benally

The interview that follows is with George Lapahie Senior. He was born and raised at Littlewater and *Tósidoh* and *Hosh*. He is 62 years old. His clan is *Taneezahnii*, and he was born for *Tódichiinii*. He went to school in Shiprock in 1945 and in *Tsé Alnaazti*. He also went to school at Chemawa, Oregon, as did Timothy Benally. He served in the military service during the Korean War. Forty years ago, he got married. He and his wife, Daisy Lapahie, have five boys and four girls and live at Two Grey Hills. His wife's clan is *Tlo'aashchioii* and was born for *Kiiyaa'aanii*. They have 26 grandchildren.

BENALLY: *When did you first go to work with uranium?*
LAPAHIE: Nineteen fifty-five when I first returned from the military service. I was looking for a job and I heard there was work there, a place called Naturita in Colorado. They were mining uranium, that is where I went. I went to work . . . in the mine. The rocks were being blasted for uranium. I was blasting the rocks where there

Fig. 6.1 George Lapahie, Two Grey Hills, 1995. Photographed by
Doug Brugge, courtesy of the Navajo Nation Museum, Window
Rock, AZ, Catalog #URC-008.B.

was uranium. The uranium would fall and it would be hauled out.
That was my work at that time.

BENALLY: *When you worked there, what was the safety of the
mining areas?*

LAPAHIE: Safety was not told to us. It was unknown to us. We
had no knowledge about safety. None. The boss would come
every week. There were two of us who were working. We blasted for uranium and then we would haul it out. That was how
it was. We went according to the way we were instructed. The
mineshaft was deep into the ground, and we did the wiring
and we hauled out the uranium and the scrap rocks. It was
quite a job because it was quite an incline from the bottom of
the mine to the top. We would get tired. We would get thirsty.
We would drink the water, which was flowing down off the
rocks in the mine. That was how we worked. We would start
work from morning to evening. Once in a while the boss

would come around. When we ran out of food, he would bring food to us again. The town is a ways off from Naturita. It must be about twenty miles. It was on the mountain in a place that was very harsh, is where I worked. Safety we did not know about, we did not know what it meant, and we never learned about it.

BENALLY: *What about the air vents? Were there any in the mines? Or was it just a mine?*

LAPAHIE: The first time that I ever worked was in 1955; at that time there were none. There was another time I worked in the '60s when there was one. It had its own hole where the vent was, and there was a long canvas tube that went down into the mine. It would blow the air out of the mine upward. I believe it also blew air down into the mine. That one was like that. They started it, and that was how it worked.

BENALLY: *When there was work, it would run?*

LAPAHIE: Yes, when we were working it ran. That was how it was when I worked over there.

BENALLY: *What company did you work for back then?*

LAPAHIE: VCA, I believe it was called. Vanadium Corporation of America in 1960; the first one was for Union Carbide, at Mt. La Sal.

BENALLY: *You were a driller, right?*

LAPAHIE: Yes, with a mine machine. I drilled.

BENALLY: *You were the ones who decided where to drill? When you were drilling it was decided by you, right?*

LAPAHIE: Yes. We just learned on our own. We were told, "This is what the ore looks like." So, when we looked for uranium, we would see narrow and wide stripes of ore. We would do blasting in the area of the wide stripes. And every [so often] they would drill from the top. They drilled from the top. Somehow they would get those big trucks called rigs. They would use that to drill down. They would tell us where the ore was, and we fol- lowed their direction and did our blasting.

BENALLY: *Yes ... you had said the boss would only come so often. Does he come on Monday to see about the work and leave right away? Does the boss come again on Friday, or does the boss come once a week? What was the time in between the visits by the boss?*

LAPAHIE: The boss would come on Monday. If he does not come Monday, he would come Wednesday. We worked on Saturday and Sunday. We did not have a day off. We worked for 30 days and then we would come home. There are two other people who came, and they worked 30 days straight, none off. When they came back, then we go up again. We worked 30 days again. So, the boss would come on a weekend, Saturday or Sunday. That is how we worked with our first boss. The other was different. They worked differently. There were more employees. Some were drivers, who hauled dirt. It was different working conditions. They drove down into the mine and hauled out.

BENALLY: *Only the food was taken care of?*

LAPAHIE: The only thing there was a shack, which was very poor, and it had a lot of spiders. [*Laugh*] There were a lot of spiders. The ones with the long legs. I don't know how many there were. But since we did not have a place to sleep, we would sleep in there. The water was water that they drilled for, spring, and we got our water from there. It was like that everywhere I worked. [*English*: The living quarters were very poor.] We brought our own food from home there. Sometimes we would run out, and the boss would buy us some meat. They provided a refrigerator, one that ran on gas. The refrigerator would just sit outside. That is where we kept our food.

BENALLY: *How many years was it that you worked with the uranium?*

LAPAHIE: Aum . . . 1955, in the months of April to September. In September the railroad [sent a letter]—I used to work for the railroad before. [*Inaudible*] Nevada, I was told there was a job position open in section six. So, we moved there in October. I went to work there until 1960, when we moved back. We had our children when we moved back, and my wife did not like being there [Nevada], too. It was difficult for the children; we had two children when we moved back. So, I made a home here for them.

There was no work around here, so I inquired for a job again. I was given a job in Utah again, on La Sal Mountain. I worked there again. In 1958, 1959, 1960 in January I was asked to come back with the railroad, and I went to Portland, Oregon. There I worked in the yard. While I was working there, I also applied for a job at PHS. I was later informed I got the job, and I took the job. I moved back and went to work for PHS. I worked for them ever since.

BENALLY: *That was in 1960?*

LAPAHIE: Yes.

BENALLY: *When you worked with the uranium, was there ever a time when you were affected by it?*

LAPAHIE: Just my ears. We used to work with the jackhammer. It was very loud. I would turn away from the noise, and today, my ears are very sensitive to the cold. The doctors look at my ears and they tell me there is nothing wrong with them. My lungs also have been collecting mucus, and I probably look normal, but in the morning when I wake up I hear it. It makes noise like *zooz*. When the mucus gets thick, I think that is when it makes noise. Just like when you drink too much coffee, it makes you nauseous, like you want to throw up. That is the way it gets me and I start coughing. When I cough, I am able to cough up the mucus and it gets better. I have told many doctors about it, and they tell me there is nothing wrong. And again when I catch a cold, and I have a cold for a while, it affects my heart. I go in for a checkup, and they tell me, "There is nothing wrong, and your heart is okay." I wonder why it is that way. I do not believe them. I am just that way now. I have to wear a sweat cap when I get cold. I think maybe they do not believe me. I wonder who really knows something about it [the cure]. If there is nothing wrong with these parts, then what is the problem? I think.

So, when my ears are hurting, it affects my eyes. It also affected my throat, and then it affects my lungs. That is my health problem. I used to really hear back then; when a child was crying in the other room, I could really hear it. Now, we are talking, I can hear and my ear catches everything that has a different voice. That was how it was in the past. And today, it is this

way. I tell people [health personnel], and they always tell me,
"There is nothing wrong with your heart; there is nothing wrong
with your ear." I think to myself when they say this, "Well, it is
good that I am okay—it is not good to have health problems."
But now it is this way. There was a woman who told me, after she
examined me, that my lungs might have clogged up from the
effects of the dust. "That is probably why you have problems
with your mucus thickening up." She had made me an appoint-
ment to do a complete examination, and I missed the appoint-
ment and it has not happened yet. That was in Shiprock. There
were other Navajos who came from Toadlena for the clinic.
Nothing ever happened for them, and nothing became of it.

BENALLY: *You do have an application in at our office [Office
of Navajo Uranium Workers], right?*

LAPAHIE: Yes. I had left one there. I was checked there
because they told me that is where you apply. They come
there from somewhere just for that, and they told me there is
nothing wrong with me. I do have the papers for that. Yes, I
applied there.

BENALLY: *Okay. You worked with the black and white people.
Washington was who they worked for in the mine. There were
many people used. The people from Washindoon knew the
health effects, but did not want the people [workers] to know
about the health effects. This is what we know today. So, there
were lies; we were used in that way. The way the Navajos were
treated in that way, what do you think about that? This is the
question. Did they do the right thing by not telling the people
about the hazards, or was it wrong?*

LAPAHIE: It is not right. It is like that all over. When I think
about it, there was no safety in it. I know this because I used to
work at Toadlena. There I worked with all kinds of detergents,
and it was hazardous. They should have told us this from the
beginning, but this was years later. We were not told of these
things. If it is not good for the people, then why weren't we told?
We were treated like this. Maybe they look at us like we were
fools and all we wanted was money—that is how they look at us.
That is the way it is. It is this way. It is like that all over. It was

not right, and we were placed in that situation, and today we are experiencing health problems. We hear that some people died from it. And so it is very difficult. We worked with a substance that was hazardous to us and we did not know it. [*English*: We have no knowledge.] We thought there was nothing wrong with it. Now when you think of it, it killed many Asians [Japanese]. I do not know how many were killed from it and burned from it. It is not good and we did not know. It looks like it is just dirt when you mine it. It was very dangerous.

BENALLY: *Yes, that is true. Because of that, the one called United States Government is now paying people back. That is what they're doing. From that time up to the present time, is the federal government working well with the Navajos? The Uranium workers? Are they saying, "This is their health problem and let's see how we can help"? Are they concerned about them?*

LAPAHIE: The one called Washington causes many hardships on the people, that is how they work with the people. I know this because I have worked with the federal government. We make everything complicated, that we cause hardship on each other. This is that way again [with compensation]. People are told there is nothing wrong with their health, even though they are really experiencing health problems. That is what I think. They [the federal government] are not working with the people right. They are not helpful. I am using my own experience, I just told you about it.

Why can't they? They are the ones who should take a close look at things, and they would know. I looked at it today on the television, and somehow they study things and they find out what it is; however, they use manipulation at its fullest. They say this is how it is, and they do not hide it when they show it. That is the only thing people are very cautious of now; the people are suspicious, they [federal government] do not work with us honestly. There are many Navajo people, who tried to get compensated and they did not get it, who have died. Some have worked for a long time and now they are gone.

BENALLY: *Okay. Next, this uranium, there is still some of it left, like in Cove and Crownpoint; they say there is a lot left. They want to mine uranium again, even in those areas where they have already mined. So here on the Navajo land, if that were to happen again, the Navajo Tribe[1] might allow it. Or maybe the Navajo people might work in that area again. Maybe they will experience health problems again. What do you think about that?*

LAPAHIE: It is obviously not good for us. I don't know. If the safety is included with the job, then it might be okay, but I don't know. [*English*: That I don't know.] The problem is, it is not good for the health. It is not good for everything. If it should happen again, yes, there is money, but it is hazardous. This makes it difficult. From that point of view, [*English*: I do not think it is any good for the Navajo Nation] to have uranium mining again.

BENALLY: *Where they had the mills and the mines, there was uranium waste left behind in piles. At the mine sites, the mines were left open and abandoned. Those places—should there be cleanup, and do you think that is possible?*

LAPAHIE: Yes, for me it is good; like I said, it is not good for us. Today, we are experiencing a great amount of problems. That is what happened to my children. They have tumor problems. What is it coming from? Through their investigation, they have traced it to the uranium. One had serious work done on his head. His skull was cut and he had radiation treatment. That is how it is. Another was affected in their internal organs. My sons and daughter are like that. Where is this coming from? In the past, there were never stories about this. Now, those of us who have worked with uranium, our children are affected by it. In Shiprock, there was a big pile of it. They used to go over there, because we used to live nearby. The houses which were on this side of it, I bought a home there. From there I went to work. They used to ride their bikes on the tailing pile to play, and now it is like that today.

BENALLY: *Okay.* [English: *You have good information.*] *Yes, that is true. The waste affects the health of the people. The women took their children with them over there to the uranium mines during the time their husbands worked there. Some of the children were born there. Those children are being affected the* *way you tell your story. It has never been really investigated before like the way we are doing now. Had several people come forth and said how it was affecting them, such as the women who followed their husbands to those places and the children who are affected—if that could be investigated . . . and made clear what was really the problem. A place to go where these people could come to be examined thoroughly and referred to the hospitals where they can get help.[2] Some of these things could and will be used in helping out those people who were affected in that way, even the children. It is that way, but this will not be until some time in the future.*

This uranium work and what has happened, how would these stories be told to the grandchildren? The important things they need to know? What it says here[3] is: [English: *What do you want the future generation to remember about your experiences with uranium? Maybe it is easier to understand in Navajo.*]

LAPAHIE: Everything, everything. [*English*: That's all. The bottom line is the money.] If there is a lot of money placed in front of us, immediately we will go for it. We will not even think about our health. We will not even think about how it will affect our health, and that it is not good for our health. After we have done it, and like I am saying now, that is what will be said, after the effects. Second, our leader is just approving things without our consent. That is our councilman. And they are only after the money, too. Another is the money to be put into the Navajo Nation. If people are informed of these things and they know about it, just like how you are both doing[4] to teach it, and they will be well informed, then it will be good. And in the future they will know that it is not good for them. Now, if it the uranium is used in a proper manner, then it can be workable again, I am sure. [*English*: There is probably a way to handle it, in a safe way.] Electricity is used like that; we use it, and it is cared for. It can harm us too if used haphazardly. It just seems that way, when I think of it.

Notes

1. The Navajo Nation banned all types of uranium mining on Navajo lands in 2005.
2. The RECA revisions of 2000 established a pulmonary clinic at the Northern Navajo Medical Center in Shiprock, addressing this concern.
3. Referring to the written interview script.
4. Referring to Timothy Benally, and to Doug Brugge, who was present and taking photographs of Mr. Lapahie.

Chapter Seven

PSYCHOLOGICAL EFFECTS OF TECHNOLOGICAL/ HUMAN-CAUSED ENVIRONMENTAL DISASTERS

EXAMINATION OF THE NAVAJO PEOPLE AND URANIUM*

Carol A. Markstrom and Perry H. Charley

There has been a proliferation of articles about disasters in the psychological and psychiatric literatures in recent years. Less apparent in these literatures is that certain groups are at greater risk for victimization by technological/human-caused disasters. In the intersection of socioeconomic status (SES) and race, people of color are especially vulnerable to contaminating conditions that compromise health and well-being

---

* This article was originally published as "Psychological effects of technological/human-caused environmental disasters: Examination of the Navajo and uranium," by Carol A. Markstrom and Perry H. Charley, in *American Indian and Alaska Native Mental Health Research: The Journal of the National Center* 11(1):19–45. Reproduced by permission of the National Center for American Indian and Alaska Native Mental Health Research.

Fig. 7.1 Mary Frank, Red Valley/Oak Springs/Shiprock, 1995.
Photographed by Doug Brugge, courtesy of the Navajo Nation
Museum, Window Rock, AZ, Catalog #URC-022.A.

(Bullard 1993). The term *environmental racism* is applied to this
phenomenon. Long-standing discriminatory practices that
have suppressed the power of marginalized groups in society
limit the ability of these groups to prevent potentially dangerous technological practices from occurring within their
domains. The same discriminatory conditions that led to such
vulnerability contribute to restricted access to appropriate
physical and mental-health care to deal with the aftermath of
technological/human-caused disasters.

   To delve into these issues more fully, and to illustrate the
effects of a technological/human-caused environmental disaster on a group in society subjected to historical racism, the
experience of the Navajo people with uranium mining and
milling is discussed, utilizing existing literature as a basis. This
article begins with various conceptualizations of disasters,
with special emphasis on the technological/human-caused

classification. The common psychological effects of disasters are briefly reviewed. The strenuous efforts for compensation are reviewed because they have been a major source of stress for families. The nature of this disaster is discussed according to impacts on the way of life and psychological well-being of the Navajo people. The article concludes with suggestions for culturally appropriate healing and recovery measures.

Conceptualizations of Disasters

Disasters can be conceptualized on a continuum of deliberateness, from "natural" on one end to "purposely perpetrated" on the other end, with the "technological/human-caused" classification between the two ends (Green 1996). A natural disaster occurs outside of the realm of human control—for example, a hurricane or a tornado. A technological or human-caused disaster is attributable to human error or misjudgment; the intent is not to cause disease, death, or disruption of lives. In contrast, a purposely perpetrated disaster is caused by a perpetrator(s) with the specific intent of human destruction (e.g., the September 11 tragedy). The technological/human-caused classification is somewhat problematic because victims may experience a mixture of benefits with adverse side effects. For instance, the introduction of an industry may provide employment and much needed income to depressed local economies, but such advantages are diminished by potentially hazardous working conditions and environmental contamination. This issue certainly pertained to the Navajo people with respect to uranium, and is discussed more fully in a later section.

Sturgeon (1993) stated, "The common theme of disasters is that they are so catastrophic and overwhelming that they go beyond anything that individuals involved normally have to cope with. As a result, their psychological capacity to function is stretched beyond the limits of endurance" (421). What is known about disasters in general is that adverse psychological outcomes can be predicted from them (McFarlane 1995). The most damaging effects of disasters can be the psychological scars of the trauma, most evident in diminished sense of safety and impaired social relations (McFarlane 1995). Adverse psychological outcomes of disasters include anxiety, depression, somatic complaints, and relationship problems (Green and Lindy 1994); substance abuse (Fullerton and Ursano 1997); and negative affect such as increased levels of anger, alienation, mistrust of others, loneliness, and isolation (Jerusalem et al. 1995).

Posttraumatic stress disorder (PTSD) is a common diagnosis with respect to disasters and frequently occurs in conjunction with other disorders, such as anxiety and depression (Green and Lindy 1994). Gender differences are apparent with PTSD. Women are more likely to experience anxiety and depression. Alternatively, men are more apt to experience alcohol abuse, physical or somatic complaints, and symptoms of hostility or acting out (Green 1996; Green and Lindy 1994). A threat to one's survival is the core of PTSD—whether it be a threat to oneself, family or friends, home, or even learning about serious injury or harm to a significant other(s) (Fullerton and Ursano 1997; McCarroll, Ursano, and Fullerton 1997). According to DSM-IV-TR (American Psychiatric Association 2000), diagnosis of PTSD is made when there has been: (a) a traumatic event, (b) a re-experiencing of the event, (c) avoidance of stimuli associated with the trauma, (d) increased arousal, (e) duration of symptoms more than one month, and (f) impairment in social, occupational, or some other form of functioning. The severity, nature, and duration of the disaster or trauma are the best predictors of PTSD. As will be shown, all are relevant to the Navajo people in their experience with uranium mining and milling.

Effects of PTSD can be acute or chronic, and chronic effects have been shown to endure for decades. For instance, with respect to the Buffalo Creek dam disaster in West Virginia, Green (1995) found symptoms of PTSD still evident 14 years later, and Honig et al. (1999) reported symptoms of PTSD 20 years later among those who were children and adolescents at the time of the dam break. Many POWs from the Korean conflict were still diagnosed with PTSD after nearly half a century (Page, Engdahl, and Eberly 1997). Additionally, an association has been found between PTSD and long-term serious physical-health outcomes among victims of severe environmental stress (Boscarino 1997). It has been suggested that with technological/human-caused disasters, some of the survivors may not return to normal levels of psychological functioning for a long period of time, if at all (Green 1996; Green and Lindy 1994; Honig et al. 1999). Long duration of psychological effects certainly applied in the case of Navajo victims of the uranium disaster, and is one area addressed in this chapter. The reader is referred to the historical context of the uranium industry among the Navajo people in chapter 3 to set the overall context.

Psychological Consequences of Uranium Disaster

Due to the unintentional but damaging environmental and health impacts of uranium mining and milling among the Navajo people, we classify it as a technological/human-caused environmental disaster. The psychological impacts of this kind of disaster can be more serious than natural disasters (Green 1996). Natural disasters are clearly evident to all people, and in response, an "altruistic or therapeutic community" emerges to help cope with the aftermath (Jerusalem et al. 1995). Such a benefit was not available to the Navajo people. The following themes of the uranium disaster give insight to the psychological repercussions: (a) human losses and bereavement, (b) environmental losses and contamination, (c) feelings of betrayal by government and mining and milling companies, (d) fear about current and future effects, (e) prolonged duration of psychological effects, (f) anxiety and depression, and (g) psychological impacts and exacerbating conditions of poverty and minority status.

Human Losses and Bereavement

Mortality risk of Navajo uranium miners was examined according to vital statistics from the years 1960 to 1990 (Roscoe et al. 1995). In examination of data from 303 of 757 miners that had died, elevated risk of mortality due to uranium-linked diseases of lung cancer, pneumoconiosis, and other respiratory diseases was reported. The loss of life among the Navajo people had a profound impact, as illustrated in the following quote by Joe Ray Harvey as he speaks of the Cove community's shared experience of grief (Brugge et al. 1997; also see chapter 9):

> There is a general sickness today, with all people.
> There are no elderly men in Cove, because they were
> mostly miners and have died, but there are many
> widows. No men! People are still suffering today,
> especially the widows. (54)

Loss of a family member, while stressful and emotionally painful, is a normal experience. However, when loss is compounded by exacerbating circumstances of disasters, bereavement can become traumatic. Trauma and loss are treated as two separate entities, but certainly can overlap in cases of disaster and form traumatic bereavement (Raphael and Martinek 1997). Not only must individuals deal with the trauma, but they also are engaged in the grieving process. Hence, traumatic bereavement is characterized by an ongoing preoccupation with the traumatic experience, accompanied by an inability to progress through the grief process (Raphael and Martinek 1997). The risk for traumatic bereavement among victims of the uranium disaster may be intensified by (a) the degree of suffering of the ill family member, (b) the premature nature of the death, (c) the knowledge that the death was due to preventable, human-caused circumstances, (d) the reluctance of any social entity to take responsibility for the disaster, (e) the number of other people in the community affected by uranium mining/milling, and (f) the reduction in household income due to illness or death of the breadwinner.

Environmental Losses and Contamination

Environmental losses are called "secondary losses" because they are widespread and affect all members of the community, whether or not they worked in the uranium mines and mills. Such secondary losses increase the number of victims of disasters and deplete much-needed coping resources and social support (Jerusalem et al. 1995). The hundreds of abandoned uranium mines and four inactive uranium mills in the Navajo Nation are evidence of the gravity of the environmental devastation. These sites continue to degrade the local environment—contaminating soil, plant life, and water, as well as the livestock that depend on clean food and water sources. Radioactive mine waste and protore were left to cause further dispersion of contaminants.

For the Navajo people, their lifestyles, traditions, and cultural practices demand a positive interaction with the forces of Nature. That is, to be in harmony and balance with one's self and with Nature. In this sense, a primary goal of the Navajo is to "walk in harmony" (*hozho nashaadoo*). This critical tie with the environment was severely disrupted by the advent of past mining practices. For instance, areas once used to gather herbs for ceremonial and medicinal properties were impacted. Areas considered sacred and linked to explicit oral traditions became desecrated from contamination.

The Navajo peoples' spiritual tie to the land overlaps with basic subsistence functions. The land provides water and vegetation for animals, and humans consume the animals, vegetation, and water. The pattern is apparent—environmental contamination has multiple routes to enter into the biological realms of humans. The Navajo people expressed concerns on all of these accounts (Woody et al. 1981). Consider the following observations by impacted Navajo informants (Brugge et al. 1997):

> *Anna Aloysious*: To this day low radiation is spreading its disease among us. They had piled up uranium ore beside the road which they never took care of completely when they left. They really did nothing in that way. They thought of us Navajo people as nothing. That's how I think about it and it really hurts my heart and mind. (28)
>
> *Dan N. Benally*: It is true that waste was dumped off the hillsides and the water carried it into the main washes. Meat from these animals is consumed, and

contamination continues to affect humans. Forty-
three of the people I worked with have died now.
Some time ago, I counted this. There are just a few
of us still around. (26)

Physical contamination also occurred through the use of
open mines for livestock pens and shelter. Radioactive stones
and protore obtained from abandoned mines were used for
construction of homes and other domestic purposes. A recent
U.S. Environmental Protection Agency (EPA) survey of water
quality of unregulated water sources used for livestock and
domestic usage indicated anomalous contamination from
arsenic, lead, and total uranium. Of great concern, as mentioned in chapter 1, was the 1979 flashflood from the rupture of
the United Nuclear Corporation's (UNC) Church Rock, New
Mexico, dam—which sent radioactive water from a tailings
pond down the Rio Puerco. The most severely affected were
1,700 people, mostly Navajo people. Children were playing in
the contaminated water, and later, only a small segment of the
population was tested for thorium, a major contaminant from
the spill (Woody et al. 1981). This incident was the largest
nuclear accident in the United States, but certainly not as well
publicized as the Three Mile Island incident (Grinde and
Johansen 1995).

The psychological impacts associated with environmental
losses can be significant. For instance, it was noted that subsequent to the Exxon Valdez oil spill, native people had higher
rates of major depression, generalized anxiety, and PTSD than
non-native people (Manson 1997). Native people subsisted on
game, fish, plants, and berries that were destroyed or damaged
by the spill. Similarly, the Navajo people are afraid of what
effects may occur from the water they drink and the animals
they consume. As summarized in Woody et al. (1981):

The residents [of the Church Rock community]
accused the companies of dwelling in "money, money,
money" while they live in fear and are faced with

questions. Where to get the next water? How to get it?
Where to graze the sheep? Whether their children
should work for the company? Whether they are
breathing radiation and who to ask for help. (82–83)

In short, lifestyles have changed due to fears of the radiation
effects on farming and ranching, and it has been necessary to
move herds to less-desirable grazing locations.

Feelings of Betrayal by Government and
Mining and Milling Companies

In addition to significant and multiple losses experienced by the
Navajo people impacted by the uranium disaster, feelings of
betrayal occurred because it was known that the adverse
impacts were human-caused and preventable. As stated by
Jerusalem et al. (1995), "Community stressors are rarely caused
by the very individuals who are forced to cope with them" (117).
Certainly there were employment and income benefits of uranium mining and milling for the Navajo Nation. However, workers
were not informed of the potential for loss of life and environmental contamination. Dawson (1992) reported that a feeling of
being betrayed by their employers was a common response by
Navajo informants. Woody et al. (1981) stated that people perceived they had been cheated, but did not know where to go for
assistance. Negative affect can be intensified by the knowledge
that a disaster could have been prevented (Sturgeon 1993). The
following comments from Brugge et al. (1997) are revealing:

Mary Frank: They did not say it was harmful, they
probably kept it a secret from us. Anglos kept that
secret—with this I think. I am very concerned because
I was left alone. (46)

Floyd Frank: Are we disposable to the government?
These are some of our thoughts this uranium brings
out to the front... (8)

Helen Johnson: The real sad thing about it was
that they were never straight about what the hell this

Fig. 7.2 Helen Johnson, Shiprock, NM, 1995. Photographed by Doug Brugge, courtesy of the Navajo Nation Museum, Window Rock, AZ, Catalog #URC-033.C.

radiation was or would do to the health of these inno-cent people. White men [U.S. government and mining companies] are not honest people.... In the treaty of 1868 it mentioned that the Federal Government would protect the health of the Navajo people. Yet they didn't do so... (36)

Betrayal also can be related to the lack of compensation from the companies and government, as described earlier and illustrated in this comment:

Paul Nakaidenae: All should be compensated, I think. We really suffered, so why is it that miners file claims and get no compensation? They have children who all are in need. (Brugge et al 1997, 27)

Fear about Current and Future Effects

There are some commonalities between the Chernobyl nuclear disaster and the uranium disaster. For victims of the Chernobyl disaster, there were three major concerns (Giel 1998): (a) the effects of current radiation on health, and whether or not current health problems were linked to the radioactivity in the environment; (b) the impact of radioactivity on the health of children; and (c) safety with respect to collecting plants in the forests, working with the land, and general food safety. In addition to current concerns of the Navajo people about safety in air, water, soil, and livestock, there is anxiety about the uncertainty about and anticipation of health effects on oneself and family. The following quotes reflect these concerns (Brugge et al. 1997; also see chapter 6):

> *George Lapahie*: Today our health is in jeopardy. My children are like that. They are experiencing difficulties health wise and are suffering. So, something called tumors are affecting them. Where are the diseases coming from? Uranium is the only culprit. (20)
> *Minnie Tsosie*: Three of my daughters are affected. They've been told that their uterus was affected. Two had their uterus removed. The other, they are still tracking her illness and she said the doctors are trying to blame the uranium. She was asked if her father worked in the uranium mines. (50)

People's fear for their offspring may not be unfounded. A study conducted among the mining population in the Shiprock, New Mexico, area demonstrated trends that lend limited support for the hypothesis of adverse genetic outcomes from radiation exposure (Shields et al. 1992). Recent efforts have been initiated through the Saccomanno Research Institute (Grand Junction), Diné College (Shiprock Campus), the University of New Mexico Cancer Research Center, and Lovelace Research Center to conduct a more detailed DNA-damage and ecological risk assessment. It is expected that what the Navajo people have feared will be empirically supported—that is, chromosomal-genetic damage has resulted from prolonged exposure to the uranium environmental hazards.

Prolonged Duration of Psychological Effects

The duration of the effects of the uranium disaster is significant because concern about the working conditions in the uranium mines were voiced as early as 1949, and the first cases of lung cancer were reported in the 1960s (Eichstaedt 1994). In our estimation, there are four factors that keep the uranium disaster in the forefront for Navajo people. First, efforts to obtain compensation by miners and millers and their families have been long-standing. Second, the environmental contamination and cleanup efforts have been seemingly endless, with no assurance of resolution in the near future. Third, there is a great deal of uncertainty and ambiguity surrounding common concerns for the health and well-being of the dependents of mine and mill workers. Fourth, there are recent efforts to resume uranium mining on Navajo trust land. Current technology and extraction methods are safer than in earlier days of uranium mining; however, based on past experiences, some people are alarmed by this prospect.

In short, the tragic aspects of this disaster have endured for four decades and have served to keep the issue alive in the hearts and minds of the Navajo people. The continual reminders may serve to increase arousal and diminish the potential for recovery. The fact that psychological disorders, such as PTSD, can endure for decades becomes especially meaningful in light of the set of circumstances just described.

Anxiety and Depression

Clearly, the uranium disaster heightened a state of transition already present in the lives of the Navajo people due to a broader U.S. culture that influenced changing lifestyles and values. The impacts from uranium mining and milling brought additional stress due to many of the factors previously described. Lifestyles were disrupted as a result of illness, loss of the primary income earner in the family, and environmental contamination that changed traditional styles of living. Changes increase stress that can lead to heightened risk for psychological disorders. However, the psychological impact of the uranium disaster has not been widely addressed in research or intervention. In the available reports, qualitative methodology was used that relied on self-report data obtained through interviews. Woody et al. (1981) examined two Navajo communities impacted by uranium mining. All respondents acknowledged deep psychological stress and despair due to trauma from the changes in their lives subsequent to their experiences with uranium. Anxiety was readily apparent throughout the comments made by respondents, and the authors speculated that this anxiety contributed to a higher degree of alcoholism on the reservation. The most prevalent theme of Woody et al. (1981), as summarized in the following quote, was that stress was induced by change due to exposure to uranium:

> The Navajo people are not opposed to change.
> However, there is often great stress related to change,
> especially when the people feel things have "gotten
> out of control" and that they do not have control over
> their destiny. This seems to be the current situation in
> the communities on which this study was based. (124).

In more recent work conducted by Dawson and Madsen (1995) among American Indian (including Navajo) uranium mill workers, 39 of 81 respondents reported anxiety, depression, or both. These emotional responses were attributed to their own health problems, the health of other mill workers, and the death of other mill workers due to exposure to uranium.

Exacerbating Conditions: Poverty and Racism

It is imperative to recognize that the disastrous effects of uranium mining and milling are among many stressors experienced by the Navajo people. When victims of technological/human-caused disasters are already marginalized due to poverty and/or racism, the impacts are compounded. Choney et al. (1995) observed that embedded in the American Psychiatric Association's description of PTSD is the consideration of threat to personal integrity. Certainly, insult to personal integrity of American Indians occurred through forced acculturation, racism, and discrimination. These and other experiences of persons from colonized groups are part of the ongoing process of historical trauma, and result in a spiritual injury called "the soul wound" (Duran et al. 1998). Manson (1997) cited the greater experience of trauma by ethnically diverse persons, and attributed this occurrence to greater stress. In particular, the complex relationship between SES, ethnicity, PTSD, and substance abuse gives an indication why some groups more than others have adverse outcomes from trauma (Manson 1997). Poverty and discrimination due to ethnic-minority status are ongoing stressors that become aggravated with additional trauma. In short, PTSD and substance abuse may not be linked to one single trigger, but are confounded through multiple stressors.

Poverty is the single most debilitating mental and physical health factor affecting individuals of any racial group, and its undesirable outcomes are well documented in the literature (e.g., Dadds 1995; McLoyd 1998; Routh 1994). In the United States, disparities in SES according to race are readily apparent (Huston 1994; McLoyd 1998; Taylor 1997), and the low SES of the Navajo population is documented in various indices. According to the U.S. Census Bureau (2000a), 40.8 percent of families with related children under the age of 18 lived below the poverty line, compared to 13.6 percent for the nation (U.S. Census Bureau 2000b). The Navajo median household income was $21,136, compared to the U.S. average of $41,994 (U.S. Census Bureau, 2000a, 2000b, respectively). Associated with lower income is the high unemployment rate of 58 percent among the Navajo people, according to the 1997 Bureau of Indian Affairs (BIA) Labor Force Report of Navajo people living on or around the reservation and considered part of the BIA Indian Service Population.

In addition to the stress associated with lower SES, the experience of racism due to inequality and restricted access to resources is a further aggravation that can lead to adverse health outcomes for ethnically diverse persons (Clark et al. 1999). Clark et al. argued that both psychological and physiological reactions to racism could lead to various adverse health outcomes, such as depression and susceptibility to physical illness.

As noted earlier, environmental racism is evident, and at a global level, traditional societies and third-world countries have been more greatly affected by environmental disasters (deVries 1995). In the United States, there is evidence of greater risk of exposure to environmental toxins for ethnically diverse populations (Pellizzari et al. 1999; Pirkle et al. 1998; Weintraub 1997) and for those of lower SES (Bellinger and Matthews 1998; Brody et al. 1994; Schmidt 1999). More specific to the Navajo and other Native nations, Churchill and LaDuke (1992) used the term "radioactive colonialism" in reference to a new form of North American colonialism directed toward technologically oriented resource extraction on Indian reservations. The stimulus for this practice is the disproportionately higher amounts of uranium, oil, gas, coal, and important minerals that are located on reservations. The irony is that these lands were not known to be resource-rich at the time reservation lands were allotted to tribes. Indeed, in many cases, seemingly the least inhabitable lands were designated for reservations.

Culturally Appropriate Intervention

We have described the specific dynamics of a technological/human-caused disaster as it psychologically impacted the Navajo people. The more pressing needs of the uranium disaster—namely, environmental cleanup and compensation—have played roles in psychological healing and recovery. However, more directed efforts toward emotional recovery are required. Three aspects of psychological intervention are addressed: (a) the role of education, (b) Diné (Navajo) conceptions of uranium, and (c) culturally specific forms of healing.

Education to Promote Understanding and Reduce Stress

Increased stress and other consequences of the uranium disaster reverberate through multiple levels of the individual, family, community, and environment. Jerusalem et al. (1995) offered a classification system for assessing community stress according to the degree of community awareness. Currently, among the Navajo people, there is a high degree of community awareness concerning the impact of uranium mining along with community efforts to cope with the problem and its aftermath, especially with respect to the treatment of environmental-contamination and compensation issues. Contamination has been, and continues to be, addressed by many organizations, such as the U.S. EPA, Navajo EPA, Navajo AML Reclamation, U.S. Army Corps of Engineers, U.S. Geological Survey, and U.S. Department of Energy.

The Uranium Education Program (UEP) at Diné College, supported by funding from the National Institute of Environmental Health Sciences and other agencies, has maintained a mission to inform people about and protect people from the risk and contamination still present in the environment. Efforts of the UEP have included (a) helping teachers develop curricula on the subject; (b) developing and distributing educational materials on environmental impacts, including water safety; (c) holding public meetings at local chapter houses to inform and educate members of the Navajo Nation; (d) pursuing community-based risk assessments (DNA-damage studies) and ecological risk assessments; (e) assisting U.S. EPA and Navajo EPA with issues of contaminated structures built with radioactive waste material from the nearby abandoned uranium mines; and (f) participating in activities related to abandoned mill sites, and attempts to clean up groundwater contamination.

In considering education and intervention with any cultural group, language issues must be addressed. There has not been a Navajo vocabulary for terms such as *uranium* and *radiological effects*. For instance, at the time of the disastrous Church Rock, New Mexico, dam break, many Navajo victims did not have a clear understanding of what occurred, or of the possible dangers. Language barriers contributed to the lack of accurate information (Woody et al. 1981). More recently, the

Uranium Education Program developed a Navajo-English glossary to describe the uranium phenomenon. Such an effort is essential to educate Navajo speakers on uranium (*leetso*) and how to protect oneself from radioactivity (*bideezla'na'alkidgo*).

Through proper education, unfounded fears can be dispelled, and anxiety levels will subsequently be lowered. Yet, appropriate cautions for safety must be maintained. Education can be a tool in emotional recovery and healing efforts. As part of education and intervention, it is essential to understand the Diné conception of uranium (also see chapter 1). Specifically, the cultural meaning of a traumatic event may be the most critical aspect determining the impact of a disaster (McFarlane 1995).

Diné Conception of Uranium

According to Navajo traditional teacher Frank Morgan (2001), the subject of uranium should be approached with an understanding of its place in the natural order and the properties it possesses. Uranium is a yellow heavy metal and has been regarded as the antithesis to the sacred corn pollen that is used to bless the lives of Navajo people. The following oral interpretation of this distinction by an informant of Eichstaedt (1994) is quite revealing:

> In one of the stories the Navajos tell about their origin, the Dineh (the people) emerged from the third world into the fourth and present world and were given a choice. They were told to choose between two yellow powders. One was yellow dust from the rocks, and the other was corn pollen. The Dineh chose corn pollen, and the gods nodded in assent. They also issued a warning. Having chosen the corn pollen, the Navajo [people] were to leave the yellow dust in the ground. If it was ever removed, it would bring evil. (47)

The Navajo people view the Earth according to four related elements of atmosphere, land, water, and sunlight/fire (Woody et al. 1981). The Earth is viewed as the female counterpart of the male Sky, and their relationship is reflected in the sphere of human existence. An ultimate goal of the Navajo people is for balance and harmony between humans and nature (Csordas 1999; Eichstaedt 1994; Woody et al. 1981). Mining is regarded as a disruption in the balance of Earth and Sky, and is disrespectful to the Earth (Eichstaedt 1994). It is believed that such a disturbance is the source of much stress experienced by the Navajo people, which ultimately has led to disease, death, and upheaval in their lives (Eichstaedt 1994; Morgan 2001; Woody et al. 1981). The fears and anxiety people hold in response to the uranium disaster are sometimes linked to their knowledge of the disruption of the Earth's elements that are reflected in atmospheric conditions, such as contamination spread through the blowing wind (Woody et al. 1981). Sadly, some of the Navajo elders blamed themselves for disruption of earth and atmosphere by permitting the uranium mining to occur (Woody et al. 1981).

Culturally Specific Forms of Healing

> Counseling helped me to express a lot of my feelings, a
> lot of the grief that I was going through, and that is
> one of the reasons why I stress that a lot of counseling
> is needed in these areas.... the victims, I and others,
> are suffering out there.

The preceding quote by Kathlene Tsosie-Blackie (Brugge et al. 1997, 40) illustrates the suffering of Navajo victims of the uranium disaster as well as a perceived need for intervention. It was observed by McFarlane (1995) that the cultural ascription of meaning to a disaster might be the strongest predictor of impact. It may follow, then, that the most effective coping strategies for dealing with disasters are culturally specific. However, the risk for societies in transition is that, due to acculturation, traditional strategies for coping with trauma are lost (Chemtob 1996). The extent to which this issue has influenced Navajo people coping with the uranium disaster is unknown. What is known, however, is that the Navajo people continue to maintain a regard for the sacred nature of the environment (Griffin-Pierce 2000), and link their own psychological well-being to environmental stability. Hence, the role of environmental restoration in psychological healing should not be underestimated.

Of paramount importance is to approach psychological healing from the impact of the uranium disaster with sensitivity. Communication patterns and various taboos of the Navajo people play roles in discussions about death and in the expression of emotions. Cooper (1998) identified communication ethics of the Navajo people according to respect, balance, containment, moderation, and reverence. There is great respect for thought and speech processes—responsibility and accountability are implicit in communication. Language is not to be wasted, and when something is spoken, it is regarded as important and meaningful. Pauses and silence in communication are comfortably permitted to allow the speakers the necessary time to prepare their thoughts. Containment, then, becomes a primary tenet of Navajo communication, because people do not share everything they know, and they think carefully before speaking their thoughts. A listener is never certain if the speaker has shared all he or she knows or thinks about a topic.

Moderation and balance also are central principles of Navajo communication, as well as behavior. Hence, speech patterns are not excessive or sensational. The inhibition of strong emotion may lead to unwillingness to discuss the death of a loved one or one's emotional distress. This is an additional factor that may contribute to the duration of psychological effects from the uranium disaster. Humor is acceptable and can be used to relieve tension and heaviness. Eye contact is avoided in order not to invade the privacy of others, and is not an evasive strategy.

Of all Navajo taboos, the one most relevant to the uranium disaster is to not speak about death or someone who has died, because by talking of the deceased, his or her ghost may be called and bring harm to the speaker (Kluckhohn and Leighton, 1948). Of interest is that in its effort to be more culturally sensitive, the American Psychiatric Association (2000) now recognizes "ghost sickness" in its glossary of culture-bound syndromes. A person may feel he/she is ill because of this sickness, which requires a traditional remedy.

A holistic view of healing dominates the belief system of many Navajo people. The interaction between the four domains of spiritual, psychological, emotional, and physical existence are recognized, and harmony between these domains is desired. The spiritual domain permeates all facets of life and needs to be implicit in intervention efforts. Nonetheless, within-group diversity exists among the Navajo people, and various belief systems operate in their lives. Csordas (1999) addressed three forms of spiritual or faith-based healing currently practiced among the Navajo people: Traditional, Native American Church, and Christianity. All three forms are regarded as resources for the Navajo people, and share a common goal that the individual acquire understanding of the philosophy that underlies the cause-and-effect nature of disease and healing. The healer must talk to the patient to facilitate such understanding. Explanations for the causes of illness may not follow Western prescriptions of pathology and treatment, but are significant within the Navajo system of beliefs. A further commonality in the three forms of spiritual-based healing is the maintenance of a holistic view of interaction between spiritual and religious beliefs and other domains of existence (Griffin-Pierce 2000).

The only Navajo indigenous form of healing is embedded in traditional beliefs. The person who adheres to the traditional belief system may have a better response when a traditional healer is involved (Choney et al. 1995; Manson 1997). The ultimate goal in this healing is to restore a state of harmony, or *hózhó*, that was upset by violations of the natural order (e.g., mining). Identifying the nature of the obstacle in the patient's life is of prime importance. In delineating Witherspoon's (1997) distinction between blessing, curing, and purifying rituals used by Navajo people, Cooper (1998) observed that cures serve to bring harmony between the patient and his or her environment (broadly defined), and bring healing in mental, physical, and environmental domains. Cures rely on both thought and speech (including singing), which are thought to have powerful capacities for restoration (Cooper 1998). In the process of healing, a diagnostician, also known as a hand trembler or crystal gazer, ascertains the nature of the illness and recommends a route for recovery. A singer will conduct a ceremony using chants and prayers to restore the patient to *hózho*. Healing ceremonies may be several days in length and require elaborate rituals, such as sand paintings, singing or chanting, and the use of holy objects (Connors and Donellan 1998).

A second form of healing practiced among contemporary Navajo people is the Native American Church, a pan-Indian movement that originated among Plains Indians around the turn of the previous century. The use of sacramental peyote and the sweat lodge are key tools in this approach. A philosophy of self-esteem predominates as the patient connects to the sacred through the use of peyote (Csordas 1999). Christian faith healing represents the third form of healing and is found in both Protestant and Catholic faiths. In this approach, the issue is one of moral identity and is based on a therapeutic principle of conversion. A unique form of Navajo Christianity has emerged, led by Navajo pastors of independent congregations. Navajo people may overlap in their use of these three healing resources, especially the traditional practices and the Native American Church, but all three forms of healing are tools in emotional recovery.

Summary

In this chapter, an attempt was made to understand a specific technological/human-caused environmental disaster in light of Navajo culture and beliefs. While the experience of the Navajo people with uranium was highlighted, the approach taken can be generalized to other groups in society. For example, chemical dumping and subsequent soil and water contamination has affected the traditional hunting, fishing, and agricultural ways of life of the Akwesasne Mohawks in both Canada and the United States (Grinde and Johansen 1995). There is concern for the health and way of life of the Inuit due to contamination of fish and marine life in the no longer pristine Arctic. Psychological disorders are more common when people face significant changes in lifestyles and experience diminished feelings of safe-ty and security. How people interpret the unsolicited changes are best understood in the complex of cultural beliefs, values, and practices. As well, steps for healing and recovery reside within these same cultural principles.

References

American Psychiatric Association. 2000. *Diagnostic and statistical manual of mental disorders (DSM-IV-TR)*. Washington, DC: American Psychiatric Publishing.

Bellinger, D. C., and J. A. Matthews. 1998. Social and economic dimensions of environmental policy: Lead poisoning as a case study. *Perspectives in Biology and Medicine* 41:307–26.

Boscarino, J. A. 1997. Diseases among men 20 years after exposure to severe stress: Implications for clinical research and medical care. *Journal of Psychosomatic Medicine* 59:605–14.

Brody, D. J., J. L. Pirkle, R. A. Dramer, K. M. Flegal, T. D. Matte, E. W. Gunter, and D. C. Paschal. 1994. Blood lead levels in the US population: Phase I of the Third National Health and Nutrition Examination Survey (NHANES III, 1988 to 1991). *Journal of the American Medical Association*, no. 272:277–83.

Brugge, D., T. Benally, P. Harrison, M. Austin-Garrison, and L. Fasthorse-Begay. 1997. *Memories come to us in the rain and the wind: Oral histories and photographs of Navajo uranium miners and their families*. Boston: Tufts University School of Medicine.

Bullard, R. D. 1993. Anatomy of environmental racism and the envi-ronmental justice movement. In R. D. Bullard, ed., *Confronting environmental racism: Voices from the grassroots*, 15–39. Boston: South End Press.

Bureau of Indian Affairs. 1997. *Indian service population and labor force estimates report, 1997*. Washington, DC: BIA.

Chemtob, C. M. 1996. Posttraumatic stress disorder, trauma, and culture. In F. L. Mak and C. C. Nadelson, eds., *International review of psychiatry*, vol. 2, 257–92. Washington, DC: American Psychiatric Press.

Chenoweth, W. L. 1985. *Historical review of uranium-vanadium production in the northern and western Carrizo Mountains, Apache County, Arizona.* (Open File Report 85–13). Tucson: Arizona Bureau of Geology and Mineral Technology.

Chenoweth, W., and R. C. Malan. 1960. *Uranium deposits of Northeast Arizona.* United States Atomic Energy Commission.

Choney, S. K., E. Berryhill-Paapke, and R. R. Robbins. 1995. The acculturation of American Indians: Developing frameworks for research and practice. In J. G. Ponterotto, J. M. Casas, L. A. Suzuki, and C. M. Alexander, eds., *Handbook of multicultural counseling*, 73–92. Thousand Oaks, CA: Sage.

Churchill, W., and W. LaDuke. 1992. Native North America: The political economy of radioactive colonialism. In M. A. Jaimes, ed., *The state of Native America: Genocide, colonization, and resistance*, 241–66. Boston: South End Press.

Clark, R., N. B. Anderson, V. R. Clark, and D. R. Williams. 1999. Racism as a stressor for African Americans: A biopsychosocial model. *American Psychologist* 54:805–16.

Connors, J. L., and A. M. Donellan. 1998. Walk in beauty: Western perspectives on disability and Navajo family/cultural resilience. In H. I. McCubbin, E. A. Thompson, A. I. Thompson, and J. E. Fromer, eds., *Resiliency in Native American and immigrant families*, 159–82. Thousand Oaks, CA: Sage.

Cooper, T. W. 1998. *A time before deception: Truth in communication, culture, and ethics.* Santa Fe, NM: Clear Light Publishers.

Csordas, T. J. 1999. Ritual healing and the politics of identity in contemporary Navajo society. *American Ethnologist* 26:3–23.

Dadds, M. R. 1995. Families, children, and the development of dysfunction. *Developmental Clinical Psychology and Psychiatry* 3:42–47.

Dawson, S. E. 1992. Navajo uranium workers and the effects of occupational illnesses: A case study. *Human Organization* 51:389–97.

Dawson, S. E., and G. E. Madsen. 1995. American Indian uranium mill workers: A study of the perceived effects of occupational exposure. *Journal of Health and Social Policy* 7:19–31.

Dawson, S. E., G. E. Madsen, and B. R. Spykerman. 1997. Public health issues concerning American Indian and non-Indian uranium mill workers. *Journal of Health and Social Policy* 8:41–56.

DeVries, M. W. 1995. Culture, community and catastrophe: Issues in

understanding communities under difficult conditions. In
S. E. Hobfoll and M. W. deVries, eds., *Extreme stress and com-
munities: Impact and intervention,* 375–93. The Netherlands:
Kluwer Academic Publishers.

Duran, B., E. Duran, and M. Y. H. Brave Heart. 1998. Native
Americans and the trauma of history. In R. Thornton, ed.,
Studying Native America: Problems and prospects, 60–76.
Madison: University of Wisconsin Press.

Eichstaedt, P. H. 1994. *If you poison us: Uranium and Native
Americans.* Santa Fe, NM: Red Crane Books.

Fullerton, C. S., and R. J. Ursano. 1997. The other side of chaos:
Understanding the patterns of posttraumatic responses. In
C. S. Fullerton and R. J. Ursano, eds., *Posttraumatic stress disorder: Acute and long-term responses to trauma and disaster,*
3–18. Washington, DC: American Psychiatric Press.

Giel, R. 1998. Natural and human-made disasters. In B. P.
Dohrenwend, ed., *Adversity, stress, and psychopathology,*
66–76. Oxford and New York: Oxford University Press.

Gilliland, F. D., W. C. Hunt, M. Pardilla, and C. R. Key. 2000.
Uranium mining and lung cancer among Navajo men in New
Mexico and Arizona, 1969–1993. *Journal of Occupational and
Environmental Medicine* 42:278–83.

Gottlieb, L. S., and L. A. Husen. 1982. Lung cancer among Navajo
uranium miners. *Chest* 81:449–52.

Green, B. L. 1995. Long-term consequences of disasters. In S. E.
Hobfoll and M. W. deVries, eds., *Extreme stress and communi-
ties: Impact and intervention,* 307–24. The Netherlands:
Kluwer Academic Publishers.

Green, B. L. 1996. Traumatic stress and disaster: Mental health
effects and factors influencing adaptation. In F. L. Mak and
C. C. Nadelson, eds., *International review of psychiatry,* vol. 2,
177–210. Washington, DC: American Psychiatric Press.

Green, B. L, and J. D. Lindy. 1994. Post-traumatic stress disorder in
victims of disasters. *Journal of Psychiatric Clinics of North
America* 17:301–9.

Griffin-Pierce, T. 2000. The continuous renewal of sacred relations:
Navajo religion. In L. E. Sullivan, ed., *Native Religions and cul-
tures of North America: Anthropology of the sacred,* 121–41. New
York: Continuum.

Grinde, D. A., and B. E. Johansen. 1995. *Ecocide of Native America.*
Santa Fe, NM: Clear Light Publishers.

Hawkhill Associates, Inc. (Producers). 1990. *Nuclear Power* (video
documentary). Available from Hawkhill Associates, 125 E.
Gilman Street, Madison, WI 53703.

Honig, R. G., M. C. Grace, J. D. Lindy, C. J. Newman, and J. L. Titchener. 1999. Assessing the long-term effects of disasters occurring during childhood and adolescence. In M. Sugar, ed., *Trauma and adolescence*, 203–24. Madison, CT: International Universities Press.

Huston, A. C. 1994. Children in poverty: Designing research to affect policy. In N. G. Thomas, ed., *Social policy report, Society for Research in Child Development*. Ann Arbor: University of Michigan Press.

Jerusalem, M., K. Kaniasty, D. R. Lehman, C. Ritter, and G. J. Turnbull. 1995. Individual and community stress: Integration of approaches at different levels. In S. E. Hobfoll and M. W. deVries, eds., *Extreme stress and communities: Impact and intervention*, 105–29. The Netherlands: Kluwer Academic Publishers.

Kluckhohn, C., and D. Leighton. 1948. *The Navajo*. Cambridge, MA: Harvard University Press.

Lundin, F. E., J. K. Wagner, S. D. Hyg, and V. E. Archer. 1971. *Radon daughter and respiratory cancer quantitative and qualitative aspects: A report from the epidemiological study of United States uranium miners*. Washington, DC: NIOSH.

Manson, S. M. 1997. Cross-cultural and multiethnic assessment of trauma. In J. P. Wilson and T. M. Keane, eds., *Assessing psychological trauma and PTSD*, 239–66. New York: Guilford Press.

McCarroll, J. E., R. J. Ursano, and C. S. Fullerton. 1997. Exposure to traumatic death in disaster and war. In C. S. Fullerton and R. J. Ursano, eds., *Posttraumatic stress disorder: Acute and long-term responses to trauma and disaster*, 37–58. Washington, DC: American Psychiatric Press.

McFarlane, A. C. 1995. Stress and disaster. In S. E. Hobfoll and M. W. deVries, eds., *Extreme stress and communities: Impact and intervention*, 247–65. The Netherlands: Kluwer Academic Publishers.

McLoyd, V. C. 1998. Socioeconomic disadvantage and child development. *American Psychologist* 52:185–204.

Morgan, F. 2001. *Cultural perspectives on radiation: "With harmony they were placed."* Workshop presented at "Creation of the Natural Order," teacher's seminar, Uranium Education Program, Diné College, Navajo Nation. July.

Mulloy, K. B., D. S. James, K. Mohs, and M. Kornfeld. 2001. Lung cancer in a nonsmoking underground uranium miner. *Environmental Health Perspectives* 109:305–9.

National Institute of Occupational Safety and Health. 1987. *A recommended standard for occupational exposure to radon progeny in underground mines*. DHHS Publication No. 88–101. Washington, DC: U.S. Government Printing Office.

Page, W. F., B. E. Engdahl, and R. E. Eberly. 1997. Persistence of PTSD in former prisoners of war. In C. S. Fullerton and R. J. Ursano, eds., *Posttraumatic stress disorder: Acute and long-term responses to trauma and disaster*, 147–58. Washington, DC: American Psychiatric Press.

Pellizzari, E. D., R. L. Perritt, and C. A. Clayton. 1999. National human exposure assessment survey (NHESAS): Exploratory survey of exposure among population subgroups in EPA region V. *Journal of Exposure Analysis and Environmental Epidemiology* 9:49–55.

Pirkle, J. L., R. B. Kaufmann, D. J. Brody, T. Hickman, E. W. Gunter, and D. C. Paschal. 1998. Exposure of the U.S. population to lead, 1991–1994. *Environmental Health Perspectives* 106:745–50.

Raphael, B., and N. Martinek. 1997. Assessing traumatic bereavement and posttraumatic stress disorder. In J. P. Wilson and T. M. Keane, eds., *Assessing psychological trauma and PTSD*, 373–95. New York: Guilford Press.

Robinson, W. P. 1998. *More than radon in the uranium dust*. Albuquerque: Southwest Research and Information Center.

Roscoe, R. J., J. A. Deddens, A. Salvan, and T. M. Schnorr. 1995. Mortality among Navajo uranium miners. *American Journal of Public Health* 85:535–40.

Routh, D. K., ed. 1994. The impact of poverty on children, youth, and families. Special issue, *Journal of Clinical Child Psychology* 23.

Schmidt, C. W. 1999. Poisoning young minds. *Environmental Health Perspectives* 107:A302–7.

Shields, L. M., W. H. Wiese, B. J. Skipper, B. Charley, and L. Benally. 1992. Navajo birth outcomes in the Shiprock uranium mining area. *Health Physics* 63:542–51.

Sturgeon, D. Posttraumatic stress disorder. 1993. In S. C. Stanford and P. Salmon, eds., *Stress from synapse to syndrome*, 421–32. London: Academic Press.

Taylor, R. D. 1997. The effect of economic and social stressors on parenting and adolescent adjustment in African-American families. In R. W. Taylor and M. C. Wang, eds., *Social and emotional adjustment and family relations in ethnic minority families*, 35–52. Mahwah, NJ: Lawrence Erlbaum Associates.

U.S. Census Bureau. 2000a. *Table DP-1. Profile of general demographic characteristics: 2000. Geographic area: Navajo Nation reservation and off-reservation trust land, AZ-NM-UT*. Available at http://censtats.census.gov.

U.S. Census Bureau. 2000b. *Table DP-1. Profile of general demographic characteristics: 2000. Geographic Area: United States.* Available at http://censtats.census.gov.

U.S. Department of Commerce. 2002. *The American Indian and Alaska Native population: 2000.* Washington, DC: U.S. Census Bureau.

U.S. Department of Energy. 1995. *Final report of the advisory committee on human radiation experiments.* Washington, DC: U.S. Government Printing Office.

Weintraub, M. Racism and lead poisoning. 1997. *American Journal of Public Health* 87:1871.

Witherspoon, G. 1977. *Language and art in the Navajo universe.* Ann Arbor: University of Michigan Press.

Woody, R. L., B. Jack, and V. Bizahaloni. 1981. *Social impact of the uranium industry on two Navajo communities.* Tsaile, AZ: Navajo Community College.

Chapter Eight

"IT WAS LIKE SLAVE WORK"

ORAL HISTORY OF MINER
TOMMY JAMES

Interview in Navajo by Phil Harrison, December 1995
Translation/transcription by Esther Yazzie-Lewis
and Timothy Benally

T he interview that follows is with Tommy James. He was born and raised in Round Rock, and lives in Cove, Arizona.

HARRISON: *When was it that you went to work in the mine? And who did you work for? When was it you first started work in the mine?*

JAMES: 1950, the last week of November, that is when the mine began over here. Well it started in July—somewhere around there. The mine had really developed when I came. But they were still faced with many problems. I came there for one main reason, and that was to get work. I had gone there to work with the tractor to build roads, because I had done that kind of work before. That work was not available, and they asked me to haul oil to the areas where they had air compressors. There were quite a few places at Mesa One and Mesa Two where they had air compressors to work with. I would haul in the morning and come back.

I repaired the jackhammer, the jackleg, and the driller. They call it "machine doctor." It was to repair jackhammers and jacklegs.

Fig. 8.1 Tommy James, Cove, AZ, 1995. Photographed by Doug Brugge, courtesy of the Navajo Nation Museum, Window Rock, AZ, Catalog #URC-017.E.

The one called jackleg, auh, is the one that held up the jack-hammer, and that is how drilling was done. I used to repair those things. I used to test them out in the mine to see if it worked, to see if it could be used again. So, I tested the machines out. That was the work I did throughout the winter. In the winter there was no road building. And when I was not too busy, I went down into the mine to help the boys and men out. I helped the miners haul out. I would use a shovel to help, or use a wheelbarrow to haul out for them. This I did because there were many elderly men who worked, and I was concerned about the elderly men. That was the reason why I helped out. When I was younger, there was nothing I couldn't do. I never thought, "This is not my job and I am not being paid for it." I did any work that needed to be done. When a person asked for my help, I helped them.

HARRISON: *What company did you work for?*

JAMES: Sidney and Delaney, they were called, who first start-ed the mining operation. Their headquarters were at Dove Creek. There is one thing I did not really learn, and that is the size of the company. There are other companies that recognize themselves as nationwide. Such as Kerr McGee. That was very clear about them. Today they [Sidney and Delaney] are not mentioned. I think it was two years, or almost two years [later], that they sold to Kerr McGee. When they sold the company, I left the job.

It was the middle of July when I was asked to haul some water in the evening when it was almost quitting time. I went for water way down below where the mountain runoff-water stream was. That same water was used for drilling in the mine. They said they ran out of water. I hauled water back up the mountain. I was hauling in an international army truck with a water tank on it. As I was hauling water around a bend one day, a vehicle came from behind the bend. When this happened, I lifted my feet off the gas pedal, and when I did this I guess the gear came out of four-wheel [drive] on the front wheels. The truck started to roll backwards with me, and I ran into a hill and the water tank fell off. I broke the water tank. It was because of this I was let go and I was fired.

This is what they did to me. In the evening when I was going home, at Cove school, AEC they call it [Atomic Energy Commission] was there. A company, which they contracted with, named Metal Engineering from Grand Junction. It was a drilling outfit. Drilling for uranium ore. They drilled in the mountains and they drilled out rocks. Core driller is what they call them. I joined them. Some of the work skills I knew were used there. I did work with tractors; that is my skill and so I applied. They told me to wait, and I started to drive the water truck. I hauled water up the mountain for drilling. About two months went by and a Cat [construction machine/road grader] was brought back. I started work with that, making roads on the mountain to the drilling sites. The core drillers were given contracts for so many thousand feet in the area. What they were given was completed and the contract finished drilling. We moved out to Colorado around November? Uravan [a place]; I left with the company.

HARRISON: *What year was this?*

JAMES: It was 1952. At that time I became a driller. There was one drill they called Syllabi that I used. I ran it. I used to have an in-law, Paul Begay's older brother. He was my helper. I worked with him. His name was Raymond. His name was Raymond Begay. It was in the springtime, like about January or February, when we moved back. We moved to Oak Springs. They had another contract in Oak Springs. All of the time when we were over in Colorado, I had eye trouble. My eyes were sore, so bad sometimes I had to go see a doctor. It did not seem like I was getting help. I would go to the doctor, and when my eyes got so bad I had to leave the company. I just let my job go. I came back here at that time, and my children's mother and I had gotten together. When I came back, I had some medicine men run ceremonies over me and I got better. In Shiprock there was some land leveling going on by the Shiprock High School, and I joined them there again. I went to work with the Shiprock irrigation and I worked with them until fall. I quit in October.

HARRISON: *At that time, what was it like in the mines? Tell us a little about it. How was it down in the mines?*

JAMES: Down in the mine, it was not like coal mining. The coal was not like strips. Coal comes in layers, but this was round-shaped and strips branching off from it. They [uranium ore] were round-shaped and strips branching off from it. Some are like that, and some do not have any branching off. It was one single round form; some were green, black, and grey. That is how it was. At night when you shine a light on the mine for a while and you turn off your light, it seems like it stayed light. It is like a watch. [*Inaudible*] Some places it smelled. The mine does smell.

There was one thing I reacted to, and that was the powder smoke. It was really bad. If the smoke was still in the air and you walked into it, it gave you a big headache. So, they did the blasting in the afternoon at the end of the workday. They have the blowers right there at the entrance. I would take the blower to the back of the mine to push the smoke out. By morning the men were put back in the mine. Sometimes the blower would stop and the smoke was still down in the mine; it was easily noticeable. That was when the smoke was not all blown out. It was easily noticeable. The smoke smells and it gives you a headache. Or you would get a nosebleed from it. That is what happened.

Some of the mines were deep, and some of the men who were working in the tunnel ended up with no air. It was said the men were falling over. At that time I was not in the mine and the tunnel where this happened; they closed it. They said, "Let's stop work for a while," and they talked to the men there, but I believe all the men were sent outside. They had the mine examined, and it was at that time they put in the surveyors to do some measuring. It must have taken almost two days of surveying. It was at that time they realized that the hole from the top needed a pipe. They put a pipe into the hole. They made a six-inch hole and they put the blower there. It was then they blew air down into the mine and the mine reopened. It was things like that—when men told their stories back then, they were telling the truth.

These companies were really alike in the work. It was like slave work. The reason why I say this is, from Red Mesa to Cove and up to the other mountain and to way over here was the boundary. The Navajo people from here would walk up the mountain. They went on foot up there, too. Some of the workers had cabins, like towards Colorado. They had showers. That was how it was. They did not have that here for the Navajo people—nothing, nothing.

HARRISON: *Did the companies tell you that this was dangerous, or they did not tell you?*

JAMES: No, they never did tell us. No. They did not say that. Today the miners have earplugs and respirators. Glasses—even though you do not wear glasses, they give you nonprescription glasses. That is how work is done today, with safety devices. That is how it is. Back then there were none. Also, there was no physical examination either, none. I did not have safety devices, no. They never discussed it either.

I said the men would walk up there; there was an elderly man who walked up there. At that time the nights were short, so I do not know when he would get started walking up there. He walked up from here and in the evening he walked back down, all on foot. I think they killed off the people just by having them walk like this. Now, Kerr McGee was the company, and they were the ones who operated the longest. That is why I am saying what I am saying. The companies never prepared anything for the Navajo workers. But for the Anglos who were surveyors, mechanics, and ones who worked in the office, they had showers for them. They had the mess hall for them. More like room and board; they had cabins for them. For the Navajo miners there was nothing, no facilities. We built our tents among the oak trees, just anywhere. It was like that for about three years.

HARRISON: *Just exactly how long did you work in the mines? Just the mines . . .*

JAMES: Three years I worked.

HARRISON: *That was underground?*

JAMES: Yes, underground.

HARRISON: *Okay. Now, as you think, do you believe it has some effect on you? The mine work you did, does it affect you or no?*

JAMES: Well, how it is, my nephew,[1] is my ankle joints, my hand knuckles, my wrist, all of sudden it seems like you have been stuck with a needle. That is how my joints get. And my neck has gotten stiff, about a month ago. My neck really hurts. It is still that way. I can't drive in town. I have to turn my whole self around, that is the only way I can turn.

HARRISON: *Is that what it is from?*

JAMES: I wonder if it is from that, and my eyes, too. It is like when the inside of the binoculars wears out and it is black. Well that is the way my eyes are from here to there. When I look around, the blur moves around with it. That is how it is. And sometimes my chest, inside the thing I breathe with, seems to stagnate. It is like you choked all of a sudden. It does that to me all of a sudden. But I am strong with my breathing, because I can walk uphill. There are others who cannot breathe, and that may be because they are having serious problems with their breathing.

HARRISON: *Now what do you think of it? The mining took place and the uranium was hauled from our land. Today what do you think of it...?*

JAMES: Well the people were compensated, but it was not enough. That is how I think of it. You came on the road. The road was worse [then], and AEC, the one I mentioned before, they repaired the road. Back then, the same road was utilized for hauling. When the company was moving out, they did nothing about the road condition. They did not discuss it. They did not look back.

HARRISON: *It was contaminated?*

JAMES: Yes. And the waste was dumped over there. The water runs right through the waste, and we use the water. That is the same stream that was used for drilling in the mines. That is the same water the people drink, too. That is how it is with us today. And we plant our garden, but it does not grow big. Years ago, before they did any mining in the mountain, when we planted, the plants would get very big, such as watermelons and squash. It is the same in Shiprock; the farm produce are small. The melons are small, just this size.

HARRISON: *How do you think the people who worked on uranium will all be [compensated], it says—right? What do you think should be done? So all people affected can be paid?*

JAMES: Well, I am sure it is difficult. Right now, the money that we worked for has been cut back, therefore, as I think, I do not think they will ever be able to pay back for the damages. I don't think so. It can't be done. And this uranium will not stop. It will continue to kill us off for a long time. I do not think it has anything to do with the compensation. It is not medicine. With money you do get medication after you pay for it, but this will not be.

HARRISON: *Yes. Okay. Next...should there ever be mining again on Navajo land? If that should be said, should they be allowed?*

JAMES: Well, I do not think so. They probably can mine it without seeing it [in situ leach mining]. Not seeing it on the surface of the ground, maybe it can be done, but it would be difficult to extract.

HARRISON: *Yes. So, you think no?*

JAMES: I do not want it.

HARRISON: *Yes. Okay ... How will the youth, as you think of it, how will the youth remember this? Is what it is saying—right? How will the youth remember this uranium work?*

JAMES: Well, this paper you talk about [book of oral histories], you should have this information given to the schools. The same should be provided to the schools to be put in the classrooms. It will happen. The students will remember it.

HARRISON: *Video should be included. Okay. The final question says, What do you think? Some say, "I should have never worked," is what they say—right? "I should have never, shouldn't have done it, darn," is what they say—right? Or others say they should help us and pay us. That is what they say, and what do you think of that? This is the last question and this is the conclusion.*

JAMES: Well it is like this, nephew: Back then, in those years, about 1946 and forward, jobs were scarce. That is how it was. You do not know where I went to get a job. I went up north; I spent two years there. When I came back, work had started here. I thought maybe I can get work and that is what happened. I got a job and I stayed around because of my work. And there is probably nothing wrong with it, but what we call life varies in length. And people have been dying off, even though they don't care how much, how important the person is. They still die. And to say I wish I did not work is impossible, because like I said, there are things that are needed. Well, it is money that is used to get what is needed, such as food and clothing.

Because of these needs, even though it may be dangerous, you will go there to work. That is how it is.

HARRISON: *Okay. This is it. You have said a lot.*

JAMES: How about the mill? Have you asked questions there?

HARRISON: [English: *You are welcome to cover a little bit on mills.*]

BRUGGE: [English: *Sure.*]

JAMES: I used to work for Kerr McGee. Four of us were laid off. The mill was ready to go into operation. Kerr McGee made the mill. They wanted to do the milling. There was a contract. I do not remember who the company was that made the contract.

HARRISON: *It was made in Shiprock?*

JAMES: Yes, it was made in Shiprock. Kerr McGee made it. It was in 1954. Yes, it was in 1954. About this time of the year [December], we were told that "You no longer work here; you're transferring out of here to a new job, to uranium mill." They said it would start operation in about two weeks. The late Jimmy Ellison [and another man,] Edward McCabe, and his son. And another was my older brother. [We were sent there to the new uranium mill in Shiprock.]

HARRISON: *What was his name?*

JAMES: Peter Deswood.

HARRISON: *Oh, him.*

JAMES: And myself.

HARRISON: *Is that Peter Deswood Senior?*

JAMES: Yes. He is a senior.

HARRISON: *Yes, and yourself?*

JAMES: Yes, and myself. And for myself, I was the front-end-loader instructor. That was my job, but the mill was not quite ready to start. There were stockpiles; I do not know how long they made the stockpiles. The stockpiles were huge, some of them as big as that mesa. I don't know where they were hauled from. Some from Monument Valley, some from around here, and another, what was it called, auh ... Ambrosia Lake, from there too. There were stockpiles way up there.

The crushers were already made. They began to crush them, and the bins were made out of, like, I'll say about 15 or 20 feet width across, and the height was about 30 feet high. There were four of them on the north end. All these were filled with ore, crushed ore, ready to go into the mill. There were two belts that extended out up there. Conveyer belts. That had been made, and there were already some men working there. The boys who were working there, I only knew a few of them. Some have died. There are only a few left, I think. So, we just cleaned up at the construction for two weeks. It was not until then the mill began running. After it started operating, we were the first department who were mixing and curing. That is what we did.

HARRISON: *That was the first?*

JAMES: Yes, that was first. Ore was coming in. There was a big old rod mill there in Shiprock. I think the rods were four by eight. The rods were stacked all around. The rods were ground and put into a mixer. They added sulfuric acid and water in the mixer. When you add sulfuric acid with water, it makes it real hot. There is only one way to mix it. I don't remember how; I think you have sulfuric acid already there in the mixer, and then you pour the water into the sulfuric acid—that is the only way you can mix it. Otherwise it just starts splashing. I think sulfuric acid goes in there and water added to it. This makes it real hot and that is how they cook it. This happens first before it goes to the bleacher. And on the bottom of the mixer there is an opening, which can be shut, and the opening comes down to the floor, and we picked up the ground ore with a front-end loader. Then on the west side of this mill, they had another house, used as storage. We dumped the ground ore in there; it was called the curing bin.

HARRISON: *That was after the sulfuric acid and water were added?*

JAMES: Yes.

HARRISON: *After that?*

JAMES: Then it goes into the curing bin. And the company did not give us anything, nothing to cover our face with. No face shield or anything like protective glasses. I already wore glasses, so I did not need protective glasses. Anything that is mixed, like concrete, they don't mix it the same. Sometimes it gets really thick, sometimes it gets really light, so it splashes. There was a time when it splashed out and I burned my face. They were small splash-spot burns, and it turned into pus, leaving scars after it healed. This is what the employees suffered from.

It was one summer that we did this, and all of my crew that I worked with [were] controlling the machine better. They were better operators of the mixer. So the employer sent me to work in the shop, and I worked there in the shop. I worked in maintenance again. As maintenance workers, we had to take care of all the mill operation. Maintenance work included repairing water pipes, stain pipes, air pipes, and natural-gas pipes because that is what ran the dryer. And that was my work again for some time. I then left with another company. I worked with them for one year. And it was two years later I went back to the uranium mill again, because they needed workers.

I worked with the sample. My work with sample was to pick up the stockpile and put it into the crusher. Every time something goes wrong, or something breaks down at the mill, we were sent into the shop at the mill to clean up the bin, all the troughs, classifier, and the tank, the agitator tank. This is where the propeller runs to do the mixing. Some propellers are rubber-coated. When the rubber coat wears off, then the metal becomes bare. When this happens, the acid eats the metal. So, when that happens, just like a flat tire on an automobile, some of the metal at the bottom, when it is eaten up by the acid, it collapses, it becomes weak—no longer firm and hard anymore. It is at that time we have to take them out and cut it open and replace the metal part. We soldered the metal part back on. But the acid does not eat stainless steel. It does not bother it. And then we recap them. We had to sleep there in the tank when we worked on it, because it took so long to repair the propeller.

And when the mill started back up, the waste was spilled out, and it formed a pond next to the mill and the waste all went into the river. When the mixer emptied out and the waste ran down into the pond, nobody went in there—they called it the "Gold Room." Inside the mill there was a storage area. The storage was on the south end of the building.

HARRISON: *It is called the Gold Room?*

JAMES: Yes, it was called the Gold Room. There was a chain-link fence around the property with a gate that had a padlock. It was padlocked all the time, so nobody went near it at all except for the people who worked there.

HARRISON: *It was restricted?*

JAMES: Yes, it was restricted. Even the camera was restricted, and unauthorized personnel. There was a guard at the main gate at all times. The workers there had a pass to get in.

HARRISON: *Okay. Then you did not know about the spill, right?*

JAMES: Yes. I tried to inquire about it. That is when they said it was hazardous, and there were many meetings about it when they were discussing uranium. Way back then we worked in the mill. They said it was hazardous. What was mixed in with the ore and how was it used, I tried asking. No one wanted to discuss it, no one. "This was mixed in it and this is why it is hazardous and it is very dangerous," they never said. They were probably suspicious that I might copy it and make it. [*Laugh*] And in the '60s, everything was dying [closing], even the mine here was dying down. So, I left in the '60s. A new job started over at Kirtland. The dam was being built. The dam was going to be built, and I applied for work there. I went that way and I worked with them. When the work ended, then I went to the mine, the coal mine.

Notes

1.   According to the Navajo relational system.

Chapter Nine

"EVERYTHING HAS BEEN RUINED FOR US"

ORAL HISTORY OF MINER JOE RAY HARVEY

Interview in Navajo by Phil Harrison, December 1995
Translation/transcription by Esther Yazzie-Lewis
and Timothy Benally

This interview is with Joe Ray Harvey. He was born and raised and continues to live in Cove, Arizona. The interview was conducted in the cab of a pickup truck as Mr. Harvey navigated a rough roadway on the way back from visiting abandoned mine sites.

HARRISON: *Just when did you start working on uranium? What month, what year did you start work with uranium?*

HARVEY: That was September 16, 1961, when I first went to work with the mine. Over in Cove. I worked for Kerr McGee. I started with the night work, the night shift.

HARRISON: *Okay... Why did you start work with uranium?*

HARVEY: The reason why I started work with it was because my older brother worked there. He became ill from it. He had an accident in the mine. He was unable to work, so I replaced him. Because I took his place, that affected his payment. He had bills, and because of my replacing him at

129

Fig. 9.1 Joe Ray Harvey, Cove, AZ, 1995. Photographed by Doug
Brugge, courtesy of the Navajo Nation Museum, Window Rock, AZ,
Catalog #URC-018.E.

work it affected his pay. I then paid off his bills, and thereafter I worked for myself.

HARRISON: *What were the names of the mining companies
that you worked for? Just briefly, one after another.*

HARVEY: Okay. I first worked for Kerr McGee. I worked for
them...almost two years in Cove. I then went to Canyon City,
Colorado, to work. The company was called C. B. Johnson
Mining Company. I worked out of Cortez, Colorado. After that I
worked for the Bennie Martinez Mining Company. I worked out
of Dove Creek, Colorado. I do not know how many years I made.
I guess about seven years. Next I worked for Union Carbide
right there at the top of Slick Rock, at Egnar. And I worked for
Shamway Dayton Mining Company for many years. And the
one called Home State I worked for, for about two or three
[years]. And also from Ogden, Utah, I worked for George Energy
Resource, a mining company. I worked there for one-and-a-half
years. The companies just did leasing on their work. Different

people took on the lease. The company I worked for was Washburn Mining Company. I worked there for many years. I worked up to August the 30th, 1981. That was my last work.

HARRISON: *Total was how many years?*

HARVEY: All of it was about 20 years. Around about 20 years is what I did.

HARRISON: *Next question is, When you first started working in the mines, what were the conditions? Some say there was no air, right? What did you notice the conditions were like in the mines?*

HARVEY: My first work was with Kerr McGee. It was like that. There was no air. We worked with hardly any air; there was a lot of smoke, and when they did blasting, there was a great deal of fire powder left in the air, and we worked in it. And the vent bag, the thing that makes the air, did not come close to where we were working. They were about 100 feet away, and maybe less than that. There was no ventilation when we worked. There was no safety. The men did not work comfortably then, too. They were forced to work. You were given instructions only once, and the next time you had to be told again, and then you were laid off. That is how the men worked. That was why the men did not speak up for themselves. They did not say anything. That is how we worked; there was no air. We used the drilling pipes with hose connected to it to generate some air. That is what we did, but we were not permitted to do that either. They told us that we were cutting the air short for the drilling. There just wasn't any air.

HARRISON: *The next question is, The companies you worked for, did they tell the workers, "This is dangerous and take care of yourselves"?*

HARVEY: Back then, in 1961, there was nothing. They did not tell us that, none. "This is dangerous, this can affect you"—they did not say anything like that. You went to work, whether you were lazy or you were having a hard time on the job. The boss would tell you, "You wanted work when you came, so work. You did not come to fuss about things." That was the way they talked to us. There was nothing said about safety.

HARRISON: *Today, the work has been done and the mining took place, and how do you think of it now? Has it affected you and did you get ill from it? Do you experience colds and fevers, and do you blame it on the uranium? Is this something you are experiencing?*

HARVEY: A little bit. Today it is sort of bothering me. My walking and breathing is lacking somewhat. When I walk a while and work hard today, I am short of breath and I can't do as much. Because of that, I easily catch a cold and flu. Today, it is that way. And when I catch the fever, it immediately puts my health back. That is how it is.

HARRISON: *Next is, The government did not handle the people right—right? What do you think of that? Is that really true?*

HARVEY: Yes, that is really true. The men were never told things, and they were just sent to work in the uranium mine. They were never told, and because of that there are many who were affected by it and they have died. Today, they are having health problems now. And furthermore, it has ruined our land, water, things, plants. It has polluted the water.

HARRISON: *There are many who have not been compensated, and they are having difficulty, right? What can be done so that they won't have difficulty, to where they all get compensated?*

HARVEY: With that, as I think of it, it has affected the people and they are having health problems and it is clear. And the regulations that are imposed should not be so restrictive that people don't get compensated. Because the people have been exposed to hazards, and they have been affected very deeply. They have scars from it. Why make it difficult for them to be compensated? That is what I think.

HARRISON: *Now, if on this land, if they decide to mine again, should they be allowed or no?*

HARVEY: No, I do not think so. Because it is not good. And it is hazardous, and it is not good for human beings. And it is not good for anyone who lives on this earth. It should not be open to mine again. NO!

HARRISON: *The children in the future, what should they remember about their mother, father, grandfather who have been*

harmed by the uranium? In the future what should they remem-
ber? . . . "We know now that it was not good for us," is what we
say, right?

HARVEY: Yes.

HARRISON: *What about the children? How should they talk*
about it in the future?

HARVEY: The children, the youth should be taught and spoken to about it, so they can learn. And by their understanding
from this, they should teach each other and talk to each other
about it. That way they will remember it in the future. And
today the youth are studying various things, so they learn and
they know about it. So, if they are taught and told, in the future
they will be aware of it, know it and remember it.

HARRISON: *Next is the final question . . . How do you think of*
it, now the people have been exposed to uranium and the mines
are uncovered and there are still waste piles? It has harmed many
people, right? What are your final comments for closure, accord-
ing to your thinking?

HARVEY: Well, the way it is with us, it seems like everything
has been ruined for us. We have been exposed to radiation.
People have been exposed to it. It has contaminated the land
and water. So, for many of us, it is a serious concern. There is a
serious concern, because of how it has affected the people's
health. We are concerned about the health problems, and the
land, too. Those who have land, farms, and water—all have
been contaminated. That is what happened and we know it. It
is clear it is that way. The water is contaminated, and the air is
the same. We talk about this for them, for those of us who
worked in it. That is how it is. The water needs to be surveyed,
all of it, get water samples.[1] All of it should be surveyed—that is
how we speak for everyone. All the springs, the ones which run
down the wash. All this we want studied. This is how we discuss
this, because it has affected all people and animals and land.

The people have been seriously hurt. And they were treated
wrong. Today, they are suffering from it. Because of that, in this
Cove area there are no menfolks. There are a lot of widows.
None. There are no men. All the uranium miners are gone. They

have all died. So, the people are struggling. The women are suffering. We speak for them, and it is very hard. We think for them,
but the Navajo people do not understand our dilemma. We
need support. This is our need. That is how it is.

The land, water, air, sheep, cows: everything has been contaminated. That is how it is. This is how we are traveling in it.
The sheep and cows are drinking the water like that, and we
eat them like that, or it is sold to others. It is transmitted on to
them. Then they become contaminated, when they were not.
These are the issues we talk about for them and think about for
them. That is why we would like some research done on it. This
is how I think of it. This is my own desire and plan. I put this
before the people and they supported me. That is how it is.

HARRISON: *Who should be asked? Some say they want to
request this of the uranium company, and others say the Navajo
Tribe, right?*

HARVEY: Yeah.

HARRISON: *Some say they want to ask the Navajo Tribe and
others like EPA whom they can work with. Who will really hear
us and help fix this problem?*

HARVEY: EPA needs to research for us, and after the findings are found out, then they need to get together with the
mining companies to do repairs. And the water that was contaminated needs to be addressed, is how we advocate for them.
Some of us do.

HARRISON: *Okay.*

HARVEY: In Shiprock, not too long ago, we had a meeting like
that. Soil and water conservation—I said that there. There was
a document that was prepared, but we will be meeting on it
again. Then we will talk about it again, we said.

HARRISON: *The same work?*

HARVEY: Yes. I talked about the way things were—everything
like the streams, and the water that runs out of the mine and
then runs down into the water, which has contaminated the
people. How it has affected them all the way up to the San Juan
River. I told them that the river is probably the same. And the
water that runs from Navajo Mine is also contaminated. I said

there is a lot, and now some people talk about it. So, should we request of EPA to study this for us? Research the water, all of it. Somewhere in Goulding that happened, and they shut off the water. The people fell into dehydration. They haul their water now. It is because of these things they have talked about it more. That is how it is.

Notes
1.   After this interview, a survey of water contamination and mine waste was conducted by the U.S. EPA and U.S. DOE.

Chapter Ten

THE RADIATION EXPOSURE COMPENSATION ACT

WHAT IS FAIR?*

Doug Brugge and Rob Goble

The 1990 RECA

The U.S. Congress passed RECA in October of 1990, and regulations were promulgated by the U.S. Department of Justice (DOJ), who had opposed the legislation, in April of 1991, with the first claims paid in 1992. While many concerns were raised about RECA, we focus here primarily on the core issue of defining who was eligible.

The act is in need of evaluation since it was in effect for ten years and was widely perceived as flawed by former miners, their families, and their advocates, as evidenced by its amendment in 2000. In particular, the questions that we are interested in are: To what extent did 1990 RECA resolve the major issues of injustice to U.S. uranium miners and why? How might any shortcomings be fixed? And what lessons can be drawn about the best way to compensate workers injured by government policies? To get to these questions, we must first examine the provisions of RECA.

---

* This article originally appeared in *New Solutions: A Journal of Environment and Occupational Health Policy* 13, no. 4 (2003): 385–97. Reprinted with permission from Baywood Publishing Company, Inc.

RECA states, "The United States should recognize and assume responsibility for the harm done to these individuals," and that the purpose of the act was to "make partial restitution." Most critically, the act says, "The Congress apologizes on behalf of the Nation to the individuals...and their families for the hardships they have endured" (Public Law 101–426, 1990). By framing the compensation program in the form of an apology, Congress explicitly set the terms for how the program would be perceived when it began denying claims. Further, the U.S. Congress wrote RECA with eligibility criteria defined legislatively, leaving little room for later administrative adjustment by the U.S. DOJ.

RECA Criteria

RECA applied not only to uranium miners, but also to residents living downwind of the Nevada Test Site at which aboveground nuclear tests were conducted, and to workers at that site—two groups that we will not examine here. The RECA regulations for uranium miners (USDOJ 1992) sought first to determine whether each individual applicant worked in uranium mining, and if they did, whether they received an exposure to radon above certain thresholds. Second, RECA required medical proof that the miner had lung cancer or a nonmalignant respiratory disease.

Exposure Data

Exposure data exist for many, but not all of the uranium mines that the former miners worked in. It was these data that were used in the prospective health studies of U.S. uranium miners (Roscoe et al. 1989). It is also these data that U.S. DOJ used to assess compensation claims of former miners. Since exposure data on individual miners were rarely if ever collected (a sharp contrast to Department of Energy workers, who wore film badges), a decision hierarchy was constructed.

U.S. DOJ looked first for measurements in the mine that the claimant worked during the relevant years. If these failed to exist, measurements in the same mine, within a few years of the worker's employment, were used. If these also did not exist, U.S. DOJ then looked at records from mines based on geographical area, seeking data first from local areas and then from larger areas, eventually resorting to statewide averages if no other data were available. Based on a comparison of radon levels derived from this schema and the work records of the former miner (time worked as recorded by Social Security multiplied by exposure levels), a personal exposure in Working Level Months (WLM, a measure of radon exposure; see Committee on the Biological Effects of Ionizing Radiation 1988, and chapter 3) was calculated and assigned to each miner (USDOJ 1992).

This decision-making process resulted in an undetermined error being associated with the assignment of exposure—and, it seems to us, almost certainly very large errors in at least some cases. We know from industrial hygiene that area measurements frequently do not reflect individual breathing-zone exposures. Thus, measurements in different mines and statewide averages can be expected to poorly approximate actual exposures.

Medical Conditions and Exposure Thresholds
Under RECA, the medical conditions that could be compensated were lung cancer, pulmonary fibrosis, cor pulmonale, and moderate to severe silicosis or pneumoconiosis as diagnosed by a qualified physician. If the miner met the medical criteria, his personal exposure was then compared to thresholds. For nonsmokers, the threshold was 200 WLM, and for smokers it was 500 WLM (or 300 WLM if lung cancer occurred under age 45).

The basis for these criteria appears to be a modification of a recommendation suggested by Victor Archer (who headed up the uranium-miner health study). In 1990, before the U.S. Congress, Archer stated that cancers in nonsmokers with exposures above 100 WLM were more likely than not due to radon, that cancers in smokers with exposures above 800 WLM were most likely due to radon, and that cancers in heavy smokers with exposures below 300 WLM were most likely due to smoking (Archer 1990).

Early versions of the legislation retained Archer's proposed thresholds (RECA 1990), which were subsequently adjusted through a political process that does not appear to have been documented (G. Fischer, U.S. DOJ, personal communication, June 2001). It is not apparent why the legislation did not draw upon BEIR IV (Committee on the Biological Effects of Ionizing Radiation 1988), a comprehensive review of the scientific literature on the health risks of radon. BEIR IV was available at the time of the hearings and might have led to setting a much lower threshold based on doubling dose, estimated at 40 WLM in their simplest model for both smokers and nonsmokers.

Smoking

Smoking was defined under RECA legislation as having smoked greater than "one pack year" of cigarettes over a lifetime (USDOJ 1992). This means that a person who has smoked any combination of cigarettes that add up to the equivalent of 20 cigarettes per day for one year (i.e., an alternative would be one cigarette per day for 20 years) was defined as a smoker. In practice, smoking status was commonly determined from the applicant's medical records. The assumption was that anyone who was listed as a smoker by his or her physician must have smoked more than one pack year due to the addictive nature of smoking. These smoking criteria were in sharp contrast to the criteria for downwinders, for whom smoking was defined as 20 pack years in the same legislation. The very large discrepancy creates an unfortunate suggestion of bias, since downwinders were community residents rather than workers, and were also predominately white, while many miners were Native American or Hispanic.

Failure on any of the criteria, absence of disease, or an exposure below the appointed threshold resulted in withholding compensation. Compensation was all or nothing. The burden was on the miner, his family, his lawyer, or his representative to prove that they satisfied the qualifying criteria. The application process was designed by Congress to prevent or severely limit payments to putatively undeserving applicants and U.S. DOJ had only limited leeway to modify its approach. If the miners or their surviving families met the criteria, then they were awarded a payment of $100,000 for each qualified miner.

Experience with RECA prior to Amendment

From April 1992 to July 2000, DOJ paid a total of 1,599 claims to uranium miners under RECA and denied an almost equal number (1,554). In addition 1,603 claims filed by downwinders were approved and 1,252 denied. There were awards for 22 cases of childhood leukemia and 19 were denied. Somewhat less successful were onsite workers, who had 211 claims approved and 741 denied (G. Fischer, U.S. DOJ, personal communication, August 11, 2000). It is unclear how many former miners may not have filed claims from lack of knowledge about the program, but it has been estimated that over 10,000 workers had been employed (Eichstaedt 1994).

Issues and Concerns with RECA and Its Implementation

The central criticism of 1990 RECA by former miners, their families, and advocates for the miners was that the law failed to compensate many deserving claims. Even assuming that the exposure estimates were accurate, which is almost certainly not the case, and using the consensus risk estimates of the time from BEIR IV, RECA criteria meant that former workers with lung cancer had to have a risk of six times normal for lung cancer if they were nonsmokers, and fifteen times normal if they were smokers. These were extremely stringent conditions for compensation. The criteria compare very poorly to the doubling-of-risk criterion that is often considered the standard for civil lawsuits (Bailey 1994). Moreover, the doubling standard might itself be considered too stringent. For instance, Hattis et al. (1995) observed that compensating DOE workers only above the doubling dose would result in only a tiny fraction of workers with radiation-induced cancer being compensated. More appropriate might be the criterion of significant contributory effect (which may be lower than a doubling of risk) used in many state workers' compensation laws (Boden 2000).

Further, the use of radon-exposure monitoring to determine eligibility is questionable in cases where the miner had silicosis or other nonmalignant respiratory diseases. Miners with silicosis were deemed eligible for compensation, but had to meet the radon-exposure criteria. Thus, a miner with medically diagnosed silicosis but low radon exposure was ineligible (Samet 1998). It is questionable whether exposure to silica dust (and diesel exhaust and other respiratory hazards) would necessarily correlate with radon exposure.

Dust levels are a function primarily of work practices such as blasting and drilling. Radon levels reflect, instead, uranium content of the ore and levels of ventilation. Indeed, Duncan Holaday, the lead industrial hygienist on the Public Health Service's study of the uranium miners in the United States, noted in 1957 the high concentrations of silica dust in the mines, and the distinction between the pattern of accumulation of silica and radon (Holaday 1957). The present-day German program for compensation of uranium miners explicitly reconstructs dust, gamma radiation, and radon exposures separately to determine eligibility (D. Koppisch, personal communication, September 2001).

Smoking as Modifier of Risk

As we noted above, the wide separation between the qualifying exposure for smokers and nonsmokers, 500 WLM vs. 200 WLM, and the high values of both thresholds did not match the consensus estimates of BEIR IV (Committee on the Biological Effects of Ionizing Radiation 1988). That document recommended the use of the same risk coefficients for smokers and nonsmokers, and estimated a doubling dose close to 40 WLM. Since most of the data used for the BEIR IV analysis came from the experience of smokers, the creation of a separate coefficient for nonsmokers to reflect a less-than-multiplicative synergism would have been to make a higher coefficient (a smaller doubling dose) for nonsmokers than the

BEIR IV value, not to make a smaller coefficient (higher doubling dose) for smokers.

Native Americans and Smoking

The designation of light-smoking miners, as were many Native Americans (Brugge and Goble 2002; and see chapter 3), as smokers based on medical records, the one-pack-year threshold, and the subsequent disqualification of their claims for failure to have more than 300 or 500 WLM of exposure have been a source of particular frustration with RECA regulations (Gilles 1997). There are two related problems with respect to the smoking classification under RECA. The first is that miners may have been misclassified. The second is that the designation of miners who smoked only one pack year as smokers is at odds with the literature, which provides clear evidence that light smoking has a much smaller effect on risk than heavy smoking. Indeed, the way that smoking has been defined in the key epidemiological studies on uranium miners was not according to numbers of pack years. Instead, the most detailed categories were delineated according to numbers of cigarettes smoked per day over a lifetime, with even low-smoking categories representing many pack years (Committee on the Biological Effects of Ionizing Radiation 1988).

Inaccuracy of Exposure Records

In the above argument, we assumed that reasonably accurate records of exposure exist, but indicted that such an assumption is unwarranted. As we have noted above, exposure data of the sort gathered for the studies of lung-cancer risk and radon exposure from uranium mining were not originally meant to be used to calculate individual risks. Indeed, the exposure data were area samples, rather than personal samples specific to individual miners. As such, the workers in a mine that had an assigned rather than measured WLM value and actual exposures that varied in some undetermined manner from the assigned value. These measurements were, appropriately, intended for use in population-based studies that pooled large numbers of individuals. The expectation in such a study is that errors in exposure assignment will be random (something that may not be true, resulting in bias) and thus affect statistical power, but not the magnitude of any association seen.

A problem arises when these values are used to determine compensation for individuals. The exposure assigned to an individual will include an error, and depending on the magnitude of the error, compensation may be granted or denied unfairly for that individual, even if on a population basis these errors tend to average out. Individual justice cautions against making mistakes that would be acceptable and unavoidable, albeit undesirable, in environmental epidemiology, and does not accept the reassurance that the "errors might average out." It is notable that no one seems to have proposed incorporating a measure of error in the exposure assessments into the qualifying criteria for RECA.

Holaday regarded the radon measurements as inadequate for determining individual exposure. He wrote, "They [the exposure monitoring results] do not represent the exposure of the miners," and that "the environmental surveys were made for control purposes, not to produce records of exposures" (Holaday 1969, 551). He went on to say that the measurements would serve the purpose for an epidemiological study in which workers were entered into fairly broad exposure categories. This is quite different from their use today as bright lines that determine eligibility for compensation.

Uncertainty

Thus RECA defined sharp thresholds for eligibility, while at the same time failing to deal with two broad areas of uncertainty. First, as noted above, there is uncertainty about the exposures (smoking and radon) in each individual applicant. There is a second type of uncertainty that we have not yet considered. This is the uncertainty in the statistical association between lung cancer and radon exposure that is found in published studies of uranium miners. We do not attempt here to calculate the magnitude of the uncertainty, but simply note that it could be calculated and was not. Calculating this uncertainty would likely affect how the threshold criteria were viewed. An approach to accounting for some of the uncertainty in making risk estimates is included in the Energy Employees Occupational Illness Compensation Program Act (EEOICPA; see below).

Other Concerns

While our primary focus is the exposure and disease relationship assumed in the qualifying criteria, this has not been the only issue raised about RECA. Other concerns raised directly to one author (DB) by former uranium miners and their advocates include the following:

1. Work that miners did after 1971 was excluded from compensation (the date that ended the U.S. government's role as sole purchaser of uranium ore).
2. Mine work done above ground was excluded (for example at the Jackpile open-pit mine at Laguna Pueblo in New Mexico).
3. Diseases, including cancers known to be associated with exposure to radioisotopes found in uranium ore, other than those of the respiratory system, were excluded.
4. Uranium mill workers were excluded.
5. There was no compensation process for family members who lived, played, and worked near, and in some cases within feet of, the mines, and were sometimes forced to abandon homes that were contaminated.
6. Cultural and physiological differences between Native American and white miners were not taken into consideration.

In addition, issues not related to compensation per se continue to plague uranium-mining communities. These include:

1. The potential for continued exposure from abandoned mines (Brugge and Goble 2002; Eichstaedt 1994).

2. Efforts to open new in situ uranium-extraction processes in Crownpoint and Church Rock, New Mexico (C. Benally, written communication; Shuey 1997; see chapter 12).

We do not explore these issues further here, but remind the reader that the larger context strongly shapes the discussion for the affected populations.

2000 Amendments to 1990 RECA

In 1999 four bills were submitted in the U.S. Congress to amend RECA and to address many of the perceived problems with the compensation process. The bills responded to the extensive and protracted grass-roots campaign that brought together urani-um-worker organizations from around the southwestern United States (Western States RECA Reform Coalition 2000). The Western States RECA Reform Coalition was based in New Mexico, Colorado, Arizona, and Utah. In September 2001, orga-nizational members included Colorado Plateau Uranium Workers, Colorado Uranium Workers Council, Navajo RECA Reform Working Group, Utah Navajo Downwinders, Northern Arizona Navajo Downwinders, Eastern Navajo Uranium Workers, Lukachukai Uranium Workers, Church Rock Uranium Workers and Diné CARE. While the four pieces of legislation had minor variations, they were largely consistent with one another. Eventually they coalesced into a single bill that passed both the U.S. House and the U.S. Senate and was signed into law by the President of the United States on July 10, 2000 (Woolf 2000).

At the end of this chapter, table 1 lists the points raised by the grass-roots activists as demands for changing 1990 RECA. Table 2 lists the amendments successfully included in 2000 RECA (Hatch 2000). It is clear that the main demands of the miners and their advocates were met, but that not all that they wanted was included. The passage of the EEOICPA on October 5, 2000, immediately after the RECA Amendments, raised the compensation under RECA to $150,000 for future beneficiaries and provided a $50,000 retroactive payment to past beneficiar-ies. EEOICPA also added reimbursement for qualified medical expenses in order to keep the compensation equal between the two programs, even though the qualifying criteria remained substantially different between the programs (Title XXXVI, 2000). Notably, the budget for RECA payments is capped, while the budget for EEOICPA payments is not.

Immediately after passage of the amendments, it became clear that the money to pay approved claims had not been appropriated and required further congressional action to be resolved. This led to the amazing spectacle of DOJ sending out IOUs. It was July 2001 before claimants began to receive actual checks (Purdom 2001), but even then funding was put under discretionary appropriations, making future funding uncertain (Horn 2001). Later that year, the Bush administration announced that it wanted to halt payments to mill workers and ore haulers until more scientific research had been done (Gehrke 2001). By 2002, however, these workers were also receiving compensation (USDOJ 2001).

Conclusions

When the government implements a compensation program, it is critical to get the apology right from the beginning. We believe that it is not possible to simultaneously apologize, set highly stringent criteria, and place the burden of proof on the victims, as did the 1990 RECA. Failure to create a responsive and compassionate compensation process makes a bad situation worse and essentially retracts the apology. Fraud, which 1990 RECA seemed designed to foil, is minimal in cases such as this and should not be the driving consideration (Michaels 1998). Rather, the larger risks are: failing to compensate deserving claims, and creating further distrust of the government. Compensation should be a positive act of redress, an act of contrition, not a miserly and bureaucratic program that views the recipients of the apology with suspicion.

Resolving the technical details will never be easy. There are problems inherent in any quantitative criteria for eligibility, and there is need for more analysis that focuses on the objectives of compensation. Assigning a numerical value as a measure of exposure is never perfectly reliable where exposure data are limited. The combined effect of using a bright line or sharp cutoff for qualification, with exposure measurement error, necessarily means that there will be denial of some deserving claims along with approval of claims from persons with disease not likely to be caused by mining. Furthermore there will also inevitably be uncertainty in the quantitative relationship between exposure and incidence of disease, so no one will know for sure what proportion of people were affected at any exposure level.

This collection of problems is inherent to any statistical formulation, although such schemes deny fewer valid claims the lower the line is set and the more a formulation explicitly takes error into account. A positive approach is needed that begins with the evidence of exposure and disease incidence; it should focus then on setting criteria that can be used to identify and include most people whose disease was likely to have been caused by their mining experience, while excluding people whose claims are implausible.

Making application procedures reasonable, and assuring that deserving victims are informed and have access to the program are just as important as the technical criteria for eligibility. Many people found the 1990 application process burdensome; such problems were particularly acute for Navajo uranium miners (Brugge and Goble 2002).

Finally, we strongly believe that it should not be solely left to the victims and to outsiders (such as ourselves) to identify failures in a compensation process designed and implemented by the party causing the injury. It is not reasonable to expect that the initial design of any compensation scheme will be perfect. But justice requires active collaboration with the persons who are seeking compensation to assure that the program is appropriate. Just as important is ongoing monitoring to assess whether or not the program is functioning as intended, and prompt adaptation of the program when problems are identified. In 2004 and 2005, the National Academies conducted a review of some aspects of RECA, which is a positive step toward evaluating the program as it was at that time.

Legislative changes proposed to RECA prior to 2000 [Western States RECA Reform Coalition, 1999].

- Navajo people living in areas downwind of the above-ground nuclear tests of the 1950s would be eligible for compensation under the compensation program for downwinders.
- Above-ground miners and mill workers would be eligible to apply for compensation.
- The dates of work that can be considered part of a claim would be extended from the old time frame of 1 January 1947 through 31 December 1971, to a new time frame: 1 January 1942 through 31 December 1990.
- The threshold for exposure to radon would be lowered from the existing 200 Working Level Months (WLM) to 40 WLM, or work for at least one year in the uranium mines or mills.
- The distinction between smokers and nonsmokers would be removed.
- The previous payment of $100,000 would be raised to $200,000 for approved claims for persons with disease.
- A $50,000 payment would be made to any uranium workers who were unethically enrolled in government studies, regardless of exposure or existence of disease.
- A $50,000 payment would be made to the families of any uranium workers who suffered death in the course of their employment that was not otherwise compensable (i.e., was not lung cancer or other diseases known to be associated with uranium mining).
- A $20,000 payment would be made to any uranium worker who suffered injury or disability that was not otherwise compensable during the course of his/her work.
- The work week assumed for exposure estimates would be based on six days instead of five.

- Work in vanadium-uranium mines would be included.
- Reasonable doubt in the cases of claimants would be decided in favor of the claimant.
- Claimants would be allowed to rely on affidavits and other documentary evidence in filing their claim.
- Persons with claims that are denied could seek administrative review by the Attorney General, and should a court set aside the denial of a claim as unlawful, the claimant would be able to receive attorney's fees and costs and 8 percent per annum on the award from the time that it was denied.
- Native American law, tradition, and custom would be taken into consideration, and traditional Indian marriages would be recognized.
- Ethnic-specific standards would be used in determining lung function.
- Tribes could request to plan, conduct, and administer the disposition and award of claims to their members.
- The amendments would be retroactive to 1990, insuring that claims filed in the past would benefit.

RECA Amendments adopted in 2000 [Hatch 2000].

- Expansion of the list of diseases eligible for compensation for downwinders and on-site workers.
- Expansion of the respiratory diseases eligible for compensation for mine and mill workers.
- Expansion of the geographic area covered by the law.
- Expansion of compensation eligibility to above-ground miners and mill workers.
- Elimination of the distinction between smokers and nonsmokers.
- Allowing for certified physician/patient documentation and appropriate tests for use in verifying a claim.
- Incorporating respect for Native American law, tradition, and custom as it applies to survivor eligibility.

- Lowers the threshold for eligibility for miners and mill workers to 40 WLM.
- Mill workers are eligible for compensation for renal cancer, chronic renal disease, and kidney tubal-tissue injury.
- Adds a grant program for community-based groups for cancer screening, medical referral, and public health education.
- A separate provision in the Energy Employees Occupational Illness Compensation Program Act increased the compensation under RECA to $150,000.

References

Advisory Committee on Human Radiation Experiments, Department of Energy (ACHRE). 1995. *Final Report: Advisory Committee on Human Radiation Experiments.* Washington, DC: U.S. Government Printing Office. October. http://www.eh.doe.gov/ohre/roadmap/achre/report.html.

Archer, V. E. 1990. Testimony to the Committee on Labor and Human Resources, U.S. Senate. February 8.

Bailey, L. A., L. Gordis, M. Green. 1994. Reference guide on epidemiology. In *Reference manual on scientific evidence,* 237–56. Washington, DC: Federal Judicial Center.

Boden, L. 2002. Workers' compensation. In Levy and Wegman, eds., *Occupational health: Recognizing and preventing work-related disease and injury,* 4th ed., 237–56. Boston: Lippincott, Williams & Wilkens.

Brugge, D. M., T. Benally, P. Harrison, M. Austin-Garrison, L. Fasthorse-Begay. 1997. *Memories come to us in the rain and the wind: Oral histories and photographs of Navajo uranium miners and their families.* Boston: Tufts School of Medicine.

Brugge, D., and R. Goble. 2002. The history of uranium mining and the Navajo people. *American Journal of Public Health* 92:1410–19.

Brugge, D., T. Benally, E. Yazzie. 2001. Uranium mining on Navajo Indian land. *Cultural Survival Quarterly* 25:18–21.

Benally, C. n.d. Written testimony submitted to the U.S. NRC, Atomic Safety and Licensing Board Panel, docket no. 40–8968-ML.

Committee on the Biological Effects of Ionizing Radiation. 1988. *Health risks of radon and other internally deposited alpha-emitters (BEIR IV)*. Washington, DC: National Academy Press.

Eichstaedt, P. H. 1994. *If you poison us: Uranium and Native Americans*. Santa Fe, NM: Red Crane Books.

Fischer, G. 2001. Personal communication. U.S. Department of Justice. June.

Fischer, G. 2000. Personal communication. U.S. Department of Justice. August 11.

Gehrke, R. 2001. White House tries to delay uranium miner compensation. *Albuquerque Tribune*, August 29, A6.

Gilles, C. 1997. Meeting with DOJ leaves many Navajos unhappy. *Navajo Times*, October 30, 10.

Hatch, O. G. 2000. Radiation Exposure Compensation Act Amendments of 2000. Statement before the United States Senate. www.senate.gov/hatch/state149.

Hattis, D. 1995. *Radiation-induced cancers in DOE and contractor employees: Implications of possible alternative workers' compensation settlement policies and assessment of the possible role of new molecular biological techniques*. Report commissioned by Ashford Associates, Cambridge, MA, under a contract with COMPA Industries, Inc. (Ref: DE-AC01–94EH89501), which in turn was under contract to the U.S. Department of Energy.

Holaday, D. A. 1969. History of the exposure of miners to radon. *Health Physics* 16:547–52.

Holaday, D. A., D. E. Rushing, P. F. Woolrich, H. L. Kusnetz, W. F. Bale. 1957. *Control of radon and daughters in uranium mines and calculations on biological effects*. Public Health Service publication 494. Washington, DC: U.S. GPO.

Horn, S. H. 2001. A sad chapter: Struggle continues to compensate uranium workers. *Navajo Times*, September 13, A6.

Koppisch, D. 2001. Personal communication: Haupterband der gewerblichen Berufsgenossenschaften. September.

Michaels, D. 1998. Fraud in the worker's compensation system: Origin and magnitude. *Occupational Medicine* 13:439–42.

Public Law 101–426. 1990. 104 *Stat.* 920, codified at *U.S. Code* 42. October 5.

Purdom, T. Domenici to ex-miners: Check "almost" in mail. *Gallup Independent*, July 20, 9.

Radiation Exposure Compensation Act filed by Rep. Brooks, 101st Congress, 2nd session, Report 101–463, April 25, 1990.

Roscoe, R. J., K. Steenland, W. E. Halperin, J. J. Beaumont, R. J.

Waxweiler. 1989. Lung cancer mortality among nonsmoking uranium miners exposed to radon daughters. *JAMA* 262:629–33.

Samet, J. M. 1998. Testimony before the Senate Judiciary Committee, Congress of the United States. October 7.

Shuey, C. 1997. Why Navajos resist new uranium mining. *The Workbook* 22 (Summer): 52–62.

Title XXXVI–Energy Employees Occupational Illness Compensation Program. 2000. October 5.

U.S. Department of Energy. 1995. *Final report: Advisory Committee on Human Radiation Experiments*. Washington, DC: U.S. Government Printing Office. http://www.eh.doe.gov/ohre/roadmap/achre/report.html.

U.S. Department of Justice (USDOJ). 1992. 57 FR 12428, Final rules for 28 CFR part 79, Claims under the Radiation Exposure Act. April 10.

U.S. Department of Justice (USDOJ). 2001. Civil Program: Radiation Exposure Compensation Program. Uranium mine claim form. http://www.usdoj.gov/civil/torts/const/reca/Tre_SysClaimsTo DateSum.pdf; accessed June 28, 2002.

Western States RECA Reform Coalition. 1999. Radiation Exposure Compensation Act. Personal communications.

Western States RECA Reform Coalition. 2000. Radiation Exposure Compensation Act. Press release. June 27.

Woolf, J. 2000. Bill may finally compensate sick Navajo uranium workers. *Salt Lake Tribune*, July 25, A1.

Chapter Eleven

"WE WILL NEVER FORGET IT"
ORAL HISTORY OF WIDOWS
MARY LOUISE JOHNSON
AND MINNIE TSOSIE
Interview in Navajo by Timothy Benally, December, 1995
Translation/transcription by Esther Yazzie-Lewis
and Timothy Benally

This interview is with Minnie Tsosie, who was born and lives in Cove, and Mary Louise Johnson, who was born and lives in Red Valley, Arizona.

BENALLY: *You both had men who you lived with, who worked [in uranium mines]. And you both knew the work they did. This you will talk about. First question is, When was the first time they worked with uranium?*

MINNIE TSOSIE: Myself, I do not know when he started working.

MARY LOUISE JOHNSON: He started working there about 1950/1951, before I was with him. He was already working when I came together with him. And he worked there for 14 years. He left it for a little while.

BENALLY: *When he worked like this and then he left work, how long was it after that his health was affected?*

Fig. 11.1 Mary Louise Johnson, Mitten Rock, NM, 1995.
Photographed by Doug Brugge, courtesy of the Navajo Nation
Museum, Window Rock, AZ, Catalog #URC-023.D.

MINNIE TSOSIE: After he left work, he got another job over
here. He worked there a while, and I do not remember how
many years. I do not remember my child [referring to Benally].[1]
Some years after that, he suddenly started having fevers quite
frequently. At night he would get feverish; he said he thought
his bones would ache. He would say that, and it continued like
that. He would get feverish and he would catch a cold. And it
continued like that for many years. There was a time when it
was like that and I never paid too much attention, until one
time I started telling him to have a doctor check him. I would
tell him that, and he would not go.

It continued like that, and he continued to work with it.
Then he went to see a doctor and he was told that the pain that
he was feeling was caused from the mine work he had done.
He was given pills and thereafter he took the pills. That made
things better for a short while, and then he would feel bad
again. Then he got worse, and it did not take long after that,

Fig. 11.2 Minnie Tsosie, Cove, AZ, 1995. Photographed by Doug Brugge, courtesy of the Navajo Nation Museum, Window Rock, AZ, Catalog #URC-023.A

not many years, it immediately brought his life down. From the time he was at his worst, it was less than a year and he died. It did not take long. In the past he was just experiencing fever and I thought it was a cold. So, when he was really affected by it [uranium], it was less than a year it took his life. He already was suspicious that it was it [uranium].

BENALLY: *He knew?*

MINNIE TSOSIE: Yes, he knew.

MARY LOUISE JOHNSON: For me [*inaudible*] he was there for three months, and he was feeling ill then. He would cough and he would say he caught a cold. I would say to him, "You probably caught a cold." I would give him cold medicine and aspirins. He knew there was something wrong. He said, "They say that it [uranium] affects you; I think that is what it is." I would tell him, "I do not think so." He would get better and then catch a cold again. Then he left there and went to Mesa Verde to work for two years. He suddenly got sick. [*Inaudible*] He really got sick and we went to the hospital. The doctors examined and x-rayed him, and immediately they told him it was it. It got worse and [*inaudible*] and it took him.

BENALLY: *She has already said that this is how it has affected her children and life; how about you, my mother?*

MINNIE TSOSIE: I think the same, my son. When my children were growing up, they were told the same thing. Today, three of my daughters are told that. They are told they have cancer inside of them. The cancer has affected them in their uterus; this is what two of them were told. And they cannot have children. They were told it was not safe for them to have children like that. My oldest daughter has been seen, and she was told that she has high blood pressure and has diabetes. She said that she was also told that there is something in her stomach, and they are thinking it to be uranium-affected. She has been asked if her father worked with it. "That is what they suspect is affecting me," she said. Also, my sons, who I was with when they were small and going to school; one of them experienced a problem with his nose. There was something that was affecting his breathing, that shut off the breathing. He still says that and is still experiencing that; when he breathes fast, it is difficult for him to breathe. I have asked [him] to go to the hospital for it, and he has not gone.

BENALLY: *What is his name?*

MINNIE TSOSIE: Robertson Tsosie. The other son, his name is Lewis, was having a problem with his ear. There was a lot of pus that was running out of his ear when his father worked in the mine. Pretty soon the pus destroyed his eardrum, he was told. And he went to Durango for it. There he had surgery on his ear, and they replaced the eardrum. That was how health problems affected the children. And then I have been hearing these things, and I thought that was the cause. We were all exposed to it. I am like that too. Just like my cousin said, my knees hurt. I get the fever at night and I become fatigued. There are other times when I am not in pain, but I am fatigued. I lose my appetite; I do not think of food. This occupies my thoughts. I think this is what uranium does, and we lived in it. It becomes overwhelming. [*Lots of noise*] One of the girls is called Linda, Linda Tsosie; the other is Betty.

BENALLY: *Linda?*

MINNIE TSOSIE: Yes. Another is Rena Yazzie [*inaudible*].

BENALLY: *Okay. The mining that took place on Navajo land, how do you think of it today?*

MINNIE TSOSIE: The way I think of it, the mining on Navajo land, they were not careful with it; if it was dangerous, it was left like that. We, as spouses, they did not tell us. Our husbands applied to work there, they went to work; it was dangerous. Why did they not tell us? This is a great concern to me. If it was dangerous, why did they leave the mines open on Navajo land and abandon them, saying there was no more work? They left them open for several years, and several people died from it. Elders and mothers did not know they drank the water down there; this is after the mine company moved out. That is what happened. Our mothers were still young, and they died. I think about these things. They should have told us that it was hazardous, and they should have closed up the mines when work was done. They should have said, I think. I wonder why they did not do that, and why they did not tell us. This is what I think. I do not like this. It really bothers me, because this is what happened to my mother.

MARY LOUISE JOHNSON: That is true. [*Inaudible*] I think it is not the leaders' decisions, but the government was the one to sign the contract and give approval. Many relatives have died . . . They were my uncles, sons, and even I am sick. Close relatives. If this mining did not take place we would not be in mourning, I think. My husband, this is what happened to him. I do not sleep at nights because of that. It bothers me. I think of it. They caused it.

Even though we were compensated. "If we are compensated maybe we will find comfort in that," we think. That is nothing. Today there is nothing; we are still in mourning. That is the way I am. My children miss him and their tears are running down. There are prayer services that are held, and they go there and they cry. Grandchildren never saw their grandfather. That is how I am. I am a mother and father, that is what I am first. That is how I am.

I am very concerned about the land and the work that was done. If that never happened, I believe [my relative] would be here, is what I think. The heart does not stop hurting; you do not forget. Every so often you remember it. That is how I am. It was in the month of May, that is when my husband died—on the 22nd was the end of his life. When that time comes around, I do not feel good. When I put flowers on his grave I feel better. That is how we are today. We continue to worry about it, and we continue to wipe our tears. We have not forgotten about it. That much I want to say again.

BENALLY: *We hear that people came back from Fort Sumner.[2] There was an agreement made, and Washington said they would take care of us. That agreement that was made back then—and thinking about it today—from the time of the uranium mining forward, is the government fulfilling their role in caring for us?*

MINNIE TSOSIE: I do not think they complied with the agreement made back then. [*Inaudible*] It is very small, someone would say "just enough to satisfy the mind." Like for children. They would ask something of you, and to satisfy all of them you would buy something that they could share. Like when you bring home food, you break it up in equal portions so they will be satisfied mentally. This is so they will not have conflict among themselves. It almost seems like that for me with this. I do not think they look out for our well-being. Yes, it is true, they compensated us, but it was not enough if the claimant was already sick.

That is what happened to us. My husband was compensated when he was sick. It was nothing. There was nothing for us, we could not get a new vehicle; [the compensation money] was given to hospital debts. There was a little he wanted to give his children, even though the children were saying that it was okay and that he should pay his hospital debts. He still gave them a little. And there was nothing left. It all disappeared here, there. He asked me if I wanted some, but I told him that it was okay if you do not give me any, because you have a lot to do with it, like hospital bills, even to Albuquerque, NM, and Mt. Rose, CO. He had bills there, and when the money came it all went to bills. There was very little left, and that which was left was used to buy the casket for him when he died. There was nothing left. To get something with it, there was nothing. That was the way it was with me. Others got vehicles with it, and for me nothing.

Hardship is encountered when your husband's life ends like that. It is hard, no one to depend on; even though you have sons, they do not think of the home the way their father thought of the home. You get really tired, because you end up thinking of all these things yourself. It drains you. You do not want food; and it is true, you cannot sleep well. That is what I am experiencing. You just cry hard and feel better. And then you take a big breath again and start moving again for your children.

It affects the children, too. It is that way with me: their minds are not right—you talk to them and they get into trouble. Those are the problems that have become a part of my life. That is how I am, and it really hurts me. He should have never worked with [uranium]. That way I would still have my husband. This would never have happened to my husband. He had just become middle-aged when this happened to him. I want to still be with him. He probably went to work because there was not other work and he had children. I think that is probably why he did that.

And if the government had really been overseeing us, we are very concerned with our husbands gone. Who will mend our homes for us when they need repair? [The government] should fix our homes for us. They opened up the uranium on us; even the water is polluted with it, and the air is polluted for us who live in the Cove area. That is what they say—and the water pipes are probably contaminated and the piped water into our homes are contaminated, and we use it. Some of the homes have stone-made fireplaces that were hauled out of the contaminated area of the mountain, and it is still in our homes.

For myself, I would like for [the government] to help us with new homes. They should build us new homes which are not contaminated. The piped water: I want them to be replaced with new water pipes, is what I think. That is how my days go by. There is no one to repair my home for me. It is that way. That is how my home is.

It puts you in a state of depression when your equal partner is gone. Life becomes bland. You go out and you have no self-worth. When you're with your spouse, you feel good about yourself. When you're alone, you feel like others just laugh at you. Even though it may not be that way. I wonder what they say about me. And no one comes to see you. There is no one who will come to you to give you encouragement and talk to you about how you should lead your children on. My son is like that; he just wishes. That is how I am.

MARY LOUISE JOHNSON: It is really that way, my aunt. It is really that way, just like the way my cousin said. As I rethink it, yes, we were compensated, but we equally distributed among our children, and some of it was paid to the attorney who worked on the case for us. What we think about is still there. Money does not establish a relationship. The people who used to relate to us are gone, and we are still very much in mourning. We think about it all the time, and we will never forget it. Just like my cousin said her situation was; it is the same way with us. We need a lot of things. The money which was paid, if we all individually got paid then we would have taken care of many things with it. Our children are pitiful when we go before the attorney, because they speak about themselves like this too.

When I was paid in Santa Fe, as the check was given to me I was told it was up to me what to do with it, they said to me. It made me think back to my husband and how he was when he was in the hospital. That all became so recent again for me. At that time I told the white attorneys, I want you to equally give my children the same amount, because at the time their father applied he said it was for the children. Not even a penny short, but equal share. It is all gone now. Money does not last. [*Inaudible*]

BENALLY: *Next, if they should want to mine uranium again some time in the future, maybe ten years from now, what do you think of that?*

MINNIE TSOSIE: [*Inaudible*] Today we are in mourning. In the future should it be that way again? It is for the safety of our children. They will in the future be saying the same thing. I think that way. It should not be done. That is how I think, my cousin. It should not be, because it has taken many people. It has taken many fathers' lives, grandfathers' lives. Today, we are encountering hardship from it. [*Inaudible*] It bothers me and it hurts my heart.

MARY LOUISE JOHNSON: I think the same thing. The children should be informed now, and they should have a good comprehension of it. Generation after generation they need to be informed really well. That would be good. And it is true that money does not greet us. If you like something nice, you need money to pay for it—if you have money and you're happy about it. But it does not establish a relationship. It is true [uranium] has taken many lives. There were some with whom we had good relationships. Our husbands loved us, and we had good relationships with them.

Even though our husbands have been paid, I think that each one of us should have been compensated. We have all been exposed to it; our children and we as mothers have been exposed to it. I think we should all be compensated. The way it is—is like just being given a dollar for the compensation. This we do not like. I am like that. It is like we were not worth anything. Many people have died, is what I think. And we are not cared for by them. They were just in it for the money, and I am sure they made a lot of money, is what we think. And in return they are giving us a hard time. [The miners] barely got paid back after great efforts have been made. The compensation is something that was barely approved, and the people got a little back. This is what I think, and the money was used for hospital bills already. Because the recipient was already sick.

BENALLY: *Okay, is there anything you would like to say that you did not say? Something that was not asked about?*

MINNIE TSOSIE: Mothers should be compensated, and if we made that request I wonder if it would be possible, is what I think. Because they have abused us too. It is true they compensated our husbands, but they failed to tell us mothers that it was dangerous. "Your husband is working with some dangerous stuff," they should have said to us. [*Inaudible*] You wonder. And our children are affected by it, as we are told. They should compensate all of us. I think that we all need to be paid back, my cousin. It is true. It was the government who did this. They did not do it carefully. It was never explained clearly. I'm sure the people that can read received it in the mail. I don't know. So, we do not know. We do not know how to read. And now we think this.

MARY LOUISE JOHNSON: It is true—today, we think we are experiencing hardship because of it. I am like that. I frequently catch a cold, even in the summertime. I say it is the uranium because they used to dump it not far from where we were at the uranium mine. I might have inhaled it then. I used to cook there and I might have inhaled it then, and now my chest hurts. My arms, too, hurt over here. It hurts now and then. Sometimes it does not hurt as bad. It is true they have not bothered us again. For myself, I have not gotten a thorough checkup. There was a time when I was told there was some [uranium] on my lungs. Just a little bit. That was about three years ago. Just thinking of it, I wonder if it is that.

I'm told that too, from the doctors. It affects my throat. My throat gets dry. My husband used to be like that. His throat used to be dry. They died in our hands. I used to think he was okay. "He is just unconscious again," I thought. That is how we are, Uncle. [*Inaudible*]

BENALLY: *Okay, my aunt, this is it, and thank you for your stories. This will be for the future. This will be viewed by future children, and [this is] how they will think of it. We vote for our leaders, and it is their discretion in the future if they say they are going to mine again. The way we are today, they say the money is decreasing and they have been trying to figure out a solution. They are in discussion of where can they find funding. If someone decides to mine again, [your stories] will be there to be used. This is what the people are saying, and they are pitiful. That is why if you approve the mining, it is not right. This is what they* *will probably say, and use this at that time. That is the purpose of this, and in the future it will be used right. And thank you, and this will be all.*

Notes

1.   In the traditional Navajo relational structure.
2.   After the relocation of the Navajo people by the U.S. government and the signing of a treaty.

Chapter Twelve

EASTERN NAVAJO DINÉ AGAINST URANIUM MINING

INTERVIEW WITH RITA AND MITCHELL CAPITAN

From the film *Homeland:*
Four Portraits of Native Action,
2005, Katahdin Foundation
Update by Chris Shuey

The following is from an interview with Rita and Mitchell Capitan, and John Fogarty, MD (U.S. Indian Health Service Hospital), all from Crownpoint, New Mexico; and Chris Shuey (Environmental Health Specialist, Southwest Research and Information Center) from Albuquerque, New Mexico.

RITA CAPITAN: In 1994, we were living a quiet, comfortable life in our hometown of Crownpoint, on the Navajo Reservation. One evening, we were here at home. Mitchell brought the paper home, as he does every day, and we both read it about two or three times in disbelief that uranium mining was to begin in Crownpoint and Church Rock. They're starting up again. Without any public hearings, the Nuclear Regulatory Commission [NRC] granted permission for the deadly carcinogen to be mined right next to Crownpoint schools and churches.

Fig. 12.1   Rita and Mitchell Capitan with son. Courtesy of Katahdin
Productions, Inc.

MITCHELL CAPITAN: I don't understand the NRC, the United
States government. Why they could do this again, why they
would have a mine like this near our community?

DR. JOHN FOGARTY: From here you can see the whole town of
Crownpoint. Mitchell and Rita live just below the water tank
there in the distance. And—as you can see—very, very close to
where the Hydro Resources, Incorporated [HRI] plans to put
the uranium mine. The NRC had granted permission for the
Texas-based company to conduct the mining with a process
called "in situ leach mining."

The mining company intends to inject chemicals down into
the aquifer, next to the community water supply. Those chemicals will leach, or strip, the uranium off of the rock into the
aquifer, creating basically a toxic soup.

MITCHELL CAPITAN: Rita started to ask me questions: "Isn't
this what you had worked before? This kind of mining, in situ
leach mining?" I said, "Yeah."

RITA CAPITAN: Mitchell worked as a lab technician for Mobil Oil in the 1980s.

MITCHELL CAPITAN: Mobil was doing a pilot project with the in situ leach mining west of Crownpoint. I worked in the lab with the engineers. And no matter how hard we tried, we could never get all the uranium out of the water, so Mobil gave up. We closed the project. This is what made me start thinking about the environment, especially our water.

RITA CAPITAN: We talked about having a community meeting.

MITCHELL CAPITAN: And we decided to do something about it.

RITA CAPITAN: We put an article in the newspaper. To our surprise, at our first meeting, close to 50 community members came to that meeting. There were so many people there, a lot of faces I've never seen before. But when we went up there to talk about it, right away we had landowners start to tell us we should stay out of their business—that's their land, they can do whatever they want. It was scary. It was humiliating. It just felt like the whole community just split.

CHRIS SHUEY: There were people who stood up and accused them of anything from witchcraft to taking food out of the mouths of their grandchildren, and standing in the way of people making lots of money off of the uranium leases.

This proposal split families. It didn't just split the community, and it didn't split clans, it split blood families.

RITA CAPITAN: We lost some friends. That's something that was real sad for us. We never wanted that to happen in our community.

There was some scary times when we were told, "Just be careful, take care of yourself." I had to really protect my family. That's one of the reasons why Mitchell and I really had to find faith, and three years ago we became members of the Catholic Church.

DR. JOHN FOGARTY: There's a few families, they own the mineral rights for their land. And in the distance, you can see the area around where the mining company is. That's owned by a few Navajo families [allottees]. Those families have been promised huge sums of money by the mining company, and they have been told that this mining process is, quote, "safe."

RITA CAPITAN: We're not fighting with landowners, allottees. We're fighting with this company.

The Mother company of HRI, Uranium Resources, have worked with this technology for 30 years in South Texas, so, that experience, that's what they're going to use here to mine uranium.

BENJAMIN HOUSE

With *in situ* mining, we drill wells. No one ever goes underground, there are no occupational hazards associated with underground mining and solution mining. In fact, our miners are electric pumps. We use natural ground water, to leach the uranium. It's brought to the surface, and what we add is oxygen, and possibly some carbonate—club soda—to the water where is re-injected into the ground.

It's safe as long as it's contained, and as you can see here in this jar it is contained.

The entire well field is circled by monitor wells.

MARK PELIZZA
PRESIDENT, HYDRO RESOURCES INCORPORATED

CHRIS SHUEY: The action of pumping dissolved oxygen and sodium bicarbonate into the rocks, the in situ leachate (ISL) method, causes that uranium concentration to increase almost 100,000 times. So you go from very high-quality, pristine water, and you make it a toxic soup. Nobody could drink it.

So, the company has to make sure that none of that stuff escapes, because it's a poison.

Because the underground ... streambeds are narrower than the distance between the monitor wells, our fear is that a leakage of the mining fluids will escape, go past those monitor wells, and never be detected.

DR. JOHN FOGARTY: We have experts and hydrologists that have shown that that contamination will reach the drinking wells within less than seven years. It will, if this mine goes through, destroy the only source of drinking water for 15,000 people.

RITA CAPITAN: We're tired of it. This time they're not going walk all over us like they did then.

MITCHELL CAPITAN: We started to organize a community group.

RITA CAPITAN: We finally came up with our name, ENDAUM, which stands for the Eastern Navajo Diné Against Uranium Mining. It was really funny; Mitchell and I, we've never, never been involved in politics or anything like that before.

MITCHELL CAPITAN: It created the public awareness.

RITA CAPITAN: And that's what people are wanting; they're wanting information.

MITCHELL CAPITAN: We try to talk about facts. HRI is feeding them the wrong information. I started to drive around in our community. I felt like I was like Paul Revere. Here comes the mining!

We need to ask the council, our Navajo Nation president: Why are we going to go do something that already has hurt our people? We need to turn that around.

RITA CAPITAN: At the end, we got more votes to oppose the mining. Pretty soon, we had a petition that went around with over 1,600 names saying "no" to uranium.

CHRIS SHUEY: Despite local opposition, the energy bills of 2001 and 2003 contain measures to revive the failing nuclear industry, and in particular, millions of dollars of subsidies for in situ leach mining.

One of the companies that would qualify under the wording of the proposed provisions right now is HRI's parent company in Texas, Uranium Resources, Incorporated. You can imagine what a grant of $10 million in a year, or $30 million over three years, what that infusion of cash would do for that company.

MITCHELL CAPITAN: We had to intervene. We had to file so many papers with the NRC and testify.

RITA CAPITAN: We filed a lawsuit to prove to the Nuclear Regulatory Commission that this was not safe.

MITCHELL CAPITAN: We told them, "Would you let this happen in your back yard? Think about it. This is the same thing. We're just protecting our land."

DR. JOHN FOGARTY: Would this happen in Santa Fe, would this happen in Manhattan, would this happen in San Francisco? No. I think this is a case of environmental racism.

This is a community that has one of the lowest incomes in the country. Many of the people don't speak English. Many of the people don't have phones to be able to call their politicians. To think that a community with so few resources has been able to stop the uranium industry, the nuclear industry—you know, it's an amazing win for grass-roots democracy.

RITA CAPITAN: I'm sorry. I don't think you could do this and at the end say that your water is going to be safe. Safe enough for our children and generations to come. We might double our piles of paper here, but that's okay. We're going to continue to fight them.

CHRIS SHUEY: If Rita and Mitchell and other people in Crownpoint had not started the ENDAUM group and intervened to stop the license, there would have been mining.

MITCHELL CAPITAN: You know, looking at the corn pollen and uranium, they almost look the same. The corn pollen is a blessing. If we bring that uranium up for quick money, it's going to destroy us.

RITA CAPITAN: With grass-roots organizing and endless legal challenges, we have been able to block the new mine for nearly a decade.

We have celebrated every victory, but with the renewed interest in nuclear power and the price of uranium rising, time may be running out for our community.

Update, Fall 2005

Two legislative actions, one at the tribal level and the other in the U.S. Congress, bolstered Navajo opposition to new uranium mining in the first half of 2005.

First, the Navajo Nation Council voted 63–19 on April 19, 2005 to adopt a new tribal statute that bans uranium mining and processing anywhere in "Navajo Indian Country." Navajo Nation President Joe Shirley Jr. signed the measure into law at the Crownpoint Chapter House on April 29, 2005. The legislation, which was backed by ENDAUM and supported by numerous Navajo communities and organizations, covers all forms of uranium mining, including in situ leach mining. In the six months after the ban was enacted, President Shirley received commitments from several members of the U.S. Congress to support the Navajo uranium prohibition, and he and the bill's principal sponsor, Council delegate George Arthur, were named recipients of regional and international environmental-protection awards for their roles in passing what is believed to be the first such law ever adopted by an American Indian government.

Second, congressional conferees agreed in June to remove $30 million in proposed subsidies to uranium-mining companies using the ISL method from the massive energy bill that was eventually passed and signed into law by President Bush on August 8. The conferees' action came in response to continued efforts by Representative Tom Udall of New Mexico to delete the "research and development" grants that he and Navajo community members believed would be used indirectly by HRI to fund development of its proposed Church Rock and Crownpoint ISL mines.

Despite the Navajo Nation's extraordinary policy decision banning uranium mining, and Congress's reluctance to subsidize ISL mining, two uranium-mining companies announced their intentions to pursue development of uranium mines on properties they had acquired in several locations in the off-reservation Eastern Navajo Agency in northwestern New Mexico, including in the Church Rock and Crownpoint chapters. The companies' heightened interest in Navajo uranium was spurred by a more than tripling of the uranium-market price in the previous three years.

Meanwhile, HRI continued pursuing final NRC approval of its Crownpoint Uranium Project, defending the safety of the project against ENDAUM's and SRIC's ongoing legal challenge of HRI's ISL mining license. ENDAUM and SRIC filed a 1,200-page brief on groundwater issues and financial surety with the NRC's Atomic Safety and Licensing Board on March 7, 2005. The brief, which was accompanied by 38 exhibits, including written testimony of seven experts, charged that (1) NRC's secondary groundwater restoration standard for uranium of 0.44 milligrams per liter (mg/L) violates the federal Safe Drinking Water Act and Atomic Energy Act because it's nearly 15 times the EPA's national drinking-water standard of 0.03 mg/L and more than 200 times the background level of uranium found in the Crownpoint water wells; (2) NRC has illegally allowed HRI to defer defining baseline water quality and the hydrologic properties of the drinking water aquifers around the mining sites; (3) HRI's plans for restoring groundwater after mining and estimating its costs of cleanup are inadequate to satisfy NRC regulations; and (4) HRI's license violates federal law because HRI failed to demonstrate that drinking-water supplies will be protected from unlawful and unsafe uranium contamination.

In mid-July, however, the board's presiding judge dismissed most of these contentions, ruling that the evidence presented by the interveners was not sufficient to warrant rescinding HRI's license. The judge ruled that conditions incorporated in HRI's license by the NRC staff provided adequate assurances that HRI would conduct pre-mining water-quality and aquifer tests necessary to demonstrate that mining fluids would not contaminate underground sources of drinking water outside the company's mining areas. The judge ordered that HRI's license be amended to lower the uranium groundwater restoration standard to the level of EPA's more restrictive drinking-water standard, but the ruling was based not on the large body of medical and scientific evidence on uranium's chemical toxicity, but largely on the grounds that neither HRI nor the NRC staff disagreed with the change. The judge also ruled, based on the testimony of one of the interveners' experts, that HRI must amend its financial-assurance plan to include $12,000 in costs associated with testing waste materials prior to off-site disposal.

In Texas, HRI's parent company, Uranium Resources, Inc. (URI)—buoyed by rising uranium prices and millions of dollars in investor cash—initiated uranium production at its new Vasquez ISL mine in Duval County, increasing its work force to at least 50 people. But the company also ran into increased citizen opposition to resumption of ISL mining at its Kingsville Dome mine in Kleberg County. Local residents asked Texas environmental officials to deny URI's request to open a new well field at the Kingsville Dome mine on the grounds that the company had not successfully restored groundwater quality at two existing well fields that had been shut down since 1999. The residents alleged, based on U.S. EPA water-quality test results, that increasing levels of contaminants in their private wells were the result of mining fluids escaping from ISL well fields located one-and-a-half miles away. URI officials, repeating an assertion they have used often in New Mexico, claimed that the private wells are contaminated by natural conditions and not by mining operations. No state decision on URI's proposed expansion of its Kingsville Dome mine had been made at press time.

THE NAVAJO URANIUM MINER ORAL HISTORY AND PHOTOGRAPHY PROJECT

Doug Brugge and Timothy Benally

This appendix reviews the Navajo Uranium Miner Oral History and Photography Project, which produced the interviews and photographs included in this volume. The booklet originally produced by the project was a 64-page soft-cover volume that contained excerpts from the interviews (Brugge et al. 1997). The current volume used as its source for oral histories those generated by the project.

The Project Concept

The goal of the Navajo Uranium Miner Oral History and Photography Project was to use oral histories and visual images to produce a book, an exhibit, a videotape (designed to accompany the exhibit), and two archives. Each of these would consist of personal reflections of Navajo people who were affected by uranium mining. Each of these products was envisioned as being available, and useful, to the affected communities. The project would be in the service of Navajo miners, their families, and their communities. The current volume is the latest product of the project.

Oral history was chosen because it lets the people speak for themselves. "Since the nature of most existing records is to reflect the standpoint of authority, it is not surprising that the judgment of history has more often than not vindicated the wisdom of the powers that be. Oral history by contrast makes a much fairer trial possible: witnesses can now also be called from the under-classes, the unprivileged, and the defeated. It provides a more realistic and fair reconstruction of the past, a challenge to the establishment account." (Thompson 1988, 6)

Unlike traditional documentaries, oral history does not lend itself to simple or convenient interpretation. Nor is it as straightforward or superficially precise as quantitative science. We saw this as an advantage since we agree with Thompson when he writes of people taking oral histories. "They find that the people whom they interview do not fit easily into the social types presented by the preliminary reading. . . . Above all they are brought back from the grand patterns of written history to the awkwardly individual human lives which are its basis" (Thompson 1988, 10).

Oral history was, of course, the first kind of history, and it still has a strong place in Navajo culture. By using a method that resonated with Navajo traditions, we could hope to produce something that was relevant to the Navajo people. We also hoped to facilitate a process by which people with little access to larger audiences could "speak" relatively directly to other Navajo people, government authorities, and the general population. We hoped that through this process, "regular" people, rather than academic "experts," could preserve their own interpretation of what uranium mining represented in their lives.

The use of video and black-and-white photography were seen as key accompaniments to the recording of oral statements. In contrast to color images, which draw the eye to bright hues, black-and-white photographs accentuate the focus on the person, particularly on the face, and emphasize expressions and mannerisms. Most of the photographs were taken immediately before, during, or directly after the interview in an attempt to capture images that retained the style, attitude, and emotion that corresponded to the oral statements.

One purpose of the project was to produce materials (principally the book and exhibit) that would serve multiple functions and have an impact in a variety of spheres. At the top of our list of reasons for undertaking the project was education. We hoped to educate both Navajo and non-Navajo audiences. Many Navajo people are familiar with uranium mining. Many more, however, live at a distance from mining areas, are too young to know first-hand, or were never told the history of uranium mining. These people were deemed to be prime candidates for our education efforts through K–12 schools, colleges, and community education.

We felt that there was also a need to spread the word beyond the boundaries of Navajo Country. It was noted that there was broad national consciousness, if also controversy, about the effects of nuclear power and the use of atomic weapons. At the same time, there was little or no knowledge about how the first steps in the nuclear cycle had damaged the health and lives of Native American and other miners, arguably one of the populations that has suffered the most from nuclear technology.

By educating a broad sector of the public, it was hoped that we could contribute to campaigns that aimed to remedy—or, short of that, at least redress—historical injustices. As part of this aspect of the project, we anticipated distribution of the book to policy makers in tribal, state, and federal government.

In general, we felt that the oral histories and images would create a valuable addition to the historical record. Although a book had already been published that documented the main historical events from a journalistic perspective (Eichstaedt 1994), our project was intended to be more accessible to people who would be unlikely to read a lengthy book. In addition, the oral-history format would put the voices of the affected people at the forefront because there would be no interpretive element.

Two secondary outcomes were anticipated. These were the use of the materials that we developed as Navajo-language teaching tools, and the identification of new environmental-research needs. The oral statements would be preserved in both

Navajo and English, and thus we thought that they should be usable by Navajo-language instructors. Because the Navajo language is being lost among younger generations, we thought there was merit in contributing to efforts to preserve it (Austin-Garrison et al. 1996).

While the project was explicitly nonscientific—that is, the interviews were subjective, and the selection of interviewees not necessarily representative of the broader population—it was felt that there was still potential for scientifically testable hypotheses to emerge out of the narratives that we would record. Anecdotal evidence is not considered helpful in terms of proving or disproving scientific questions, but interesting and testable questions are frequently generated as a result of listening to community or individual concerns.

Reported next is the method that we employed for the project. There are good reasons for describing our process in some detail. First and foremost, the project design may be replicable. The generally successful outcomes that we report later in this appendix are due in large part to the approach that we chose. Second, it is our sense that the area of university collaborations with communities, and in particular communities of color, is one that is rapidly growing (Brugge and Hynes 2005). This means that many projects are being conducted in many different ways. Our reported methods will contribute to documenting these attempts. Finally, it will likely be of interest to others who have done or are contemplating similar projects, perhaps using a different method, to compare their approach with ours.

Project Method

We developed methods that seemed likely to produce results consistent with our goals. The overall framework was community-based participatory research. In this case, the university was Tufts University School of Medicine, and the community was a pool of individuals, community organizations, and tribal agencies within the Navajo Nation. Over the course of the project, our advisory board grew to 20 members, the majority of whom were Navajo people.

The project was seen as a supplement to and expansion of existing work by Navajo people to address the issue. The Navajo Nation Office of Navajo Uranium Workers (ONUW), the grassroots organization Uranium Radiation Victims Committee (URVC), and Diné College (formerly Navajo Community College) were the central groups that contributed to the collection of interviews and their processing into the booklet, exhibit, video, and archives. The Tufts Institutional Review Board approved the project, the Indian Health Service Institutional Review Board declined review after being approached, and the Navajo Nation Historic Preservation Department issued an ethnographic permit.

Proposals were written and funding obtained from four main sources (U.S. EPA, the Ruth Mott Fund, the Ford Foundation, and the Education Foundation of America). In addition, hundreds of small donations from supportive individuals were received over the course of the project. Combined funding was just over $100,000 spread over three to four years. A majority of the budget was for program expenses such as travel, printing, and the like. Budgets divided funds for salaries fairly equally between the university-based director (Doug Brugge) and consultants (primarily Timothy Benally and Phil Harrison), who were the Navajo partners. The university partner did the grant writing and administered and coordinated the overall project. Prorating compensation on the basis of time spent on the project, Navajo consultants were paid higher rates (income per unit of time worked), while the director invested a greater amount of time. The director and most of the consultants to the project also contributed varying amounts of volunteer time.

Timothy Benally (then director of the ONUW) and Phil Harrison (URVC) conducted the interviews. Each selected potential interviewees. Benally sought out individuals whom he did not necessarily know previously and who lived in outlying locations around the Four Corners area. Harrison interviewed primarily people from the Cove/Red Valley region in which he grew up. Helen Johnson (ONUW) recruited some interviewees, and Chenoa Bah Stilwell (a student at the University of New Mexico) conducted one interview that was included in the book and exhibit. Doug Brugge took the photographs.

The majority of 25 interviews (23) were conducted in Navajo. Most (22) were interviews of individuals; three were interviews of pairs. Persons interviewed were primarily former miners (16), and wives (2) or widows (7) of miners. A few daughters (3) of deceased miners were also interviewed. Interviewees were paid a small stipend and assured that they would receive a copy of the book and updates about the project. Our objective was to include the perspective not only of the workers themselves, but also of family members whose lives were affected by the experience of the miners. Interviewees who were related to deceased miners gave the most emotionally charged interviews.

All of the interviews were audio-recorded using a lapel mike, and a small subset (6) of the interviews were videotaped as well. A bilingual Navajo panel was recruited to review the audiotapes and make recommendations about which parts of the interviews to use. Benally translated the bulk of the interviews, while Martha Austin-Garrison and Lydia Fasthorse-Begay transcribed the tapes into written Navajo. Austin-Garrison's translation of one of the interviews was used in the book and exhibit. Esther Yazzie-Lewis subsequently completed, refined, and edited the full transcripts that appear as chapters in this book.

Grant funding allowed us to self-publish the booklet and distribute the majority of copies for free. Grants also paid for the production of large-format prints of the photographs for use in the exhibit. In addition, the exhibit tour was subsidized by donations, and then by a grant that allowed for professional showings. We wanted the exhibit, like the book, to be accessible to populations that would not be able to afford a commercial production. We were also asked by multiple persons during the interviews to assure that royalties, if any, would come back to the mining communities.

The video was a special and somewhat separate aspect of the project. It was initiated solely with funds drawn from private contributors, and with a completely volunteer team drawn from two UNM students (Chenoa Bah Stilwell and Katherine Bomboy) and a video producer from Chicago (Mary Elsner). After the first field shoot, funding was obtained that provided adequate support for finishing the taping and editing the final videotape, which premiered at the 1997 Navajo Studies Conference in Albuquerque, New Mexico.

Outcomes

The interviews and photographs proved to be rich in both content and tone. The interviews contained an expressiveness that provided not only factual information to those who read them, but also emotional content, cultural context, and personal style.

The Booklet

Perhaps the most visible result of the project to date has been the widespread dissemination of the booklet. We printed 2,000 copies in 1997; 2,000 in 1998; and another 1,500 in 2000. All of the first two printings and most of the third have been distributed (see table 1), and the majority were provided free of charge. Free copies of the booklet have been targeted to Navajo audiences. The largest number were given to people in the mining communities around or near Shiprock, New Mexico. The Uranium Education Center at Diné College in Shiprock coproduced the second printing in conjunction with the project, and is distributing 900 copies of the book from that printing.

TABLE 1 **Distribution of books to Navajo audiences**

Persons interviewed for the project and their families
Other former mine and mill workers
Community residents in mining areas
Community residents in areas targeted for new mining activities (Crownpoint, NM)
Navajo Environmental Protection Agency
Tribal councilors
K–12 schools
The tribal college
On sale for a time at the Navajo Nation Museum gift shop

Navajo communities have shown great interest because they were heavily affected by uranium mining, and because the booklet records the images and words of people that many community members know personally. By late 1998, Dan Crank, an advisory-board member, reported that he was distributing the book to health-care workers in Kayenta, a former uranium-mining area on the Navajo Nation far from Shiprock. Crank reports that the people he approached "really embraced the book."

Copies have also been given to schools and colleges in the Navajo Nation. Kathlene Tsosie, who was interviewed for the book, took the lead on distribution to the Navajo community of Crownpoint, New Mexico. This is the community that is grappling with the choice of whether or not to allow new "leachate" uranium mining (see chapter 12). We believe that few, if any, other environmental publications based on the knowledge of the Navajo people have been so accessible to the Navajo people. Indeed, the free dissemination of the book is at odds with the approach taken by the vast majority of publications about the Navajo people, which are frequently scholarly, expensive, or in the case of journal articles, difficult to access.

The two Navajo reviewers of the booklet both came to favorable conclusions (Crank 1997; Smith 1997). One wrote about looking first at the images and then reading the text:

> The Navajo men and women . . . were photographed in
> positions of telling their stories from their heart and
> soul. . . . Their facial lines, their hand gestures, their
> intense eyes glowing—all these and more [provide a]
> nonverbal map of Navajo uranium experiences [and]
> bring harsh reality to something that we had deemed
> happened years ago, before our times. . . . The second
> choice I had was to read the interviews either in
> Navajo or English. Like many others I had learned to
> read English first; after finishing each page in English,
> I began to read the Navajo translations. The book's
> bilingual approach does justice to the stories.
> (Crank 1997, 8).

Non-Navajo recipients of the booklet included all of the contributors of small donations to the project (table 2). These
were professors, community and environmental activists,
lawyers, physicians, and students. The booklet has been provided to members of the National Environmental Justice
Advisory Council to the U.S. EPA, and to federal officials in
the U.S. Department of Justice, Environmental Protection
Agency, and Department of Energy. It has reached Australian
aboriginal people opposed to a uranium mine where they live,
and members of a wide range of Native American tribes from
across the United States. Requests soon began filtering in
unsolicited from students and others around the country who,
having heard of the project, wanted to learn more about it.
Several book-locating services began sending requests for
copies on a regular if infrequent basis. In 2005, despite no
active advertising and the passage of years since the last printing, requests for the booklet continued at a pace of one to
three per month.

TABLE 2 Distribution of books to non-Navajo audiences

Financial contributors to the project
U.S. Environmental Protection Agency
National Environmental Justice Advisory Council to the U.S. EPA
U.S. Department of Justice
U.S. Department of Energy
Agency for Toxic Substance and Disease Registry, U.S. Centers for Disease Control
Tribal (other than Navajo) government officials
Australian aboriginal environmental groups
Anti-nuclear organizations
Some libraries
Newspapers as far away as Japan and Siberia

Efforts to target a broader sector of policy makers, including
elected officials, were undertaken in conjunction with a growing campaign to reform the federal compensation process for
uranium miners and their next of kin (the Radiation Exposure

Compensation Act, administered by U.S. DOJ). For example, one interviewee, Kathlene Tsosie-Blackie, distributed copies to the offices of congressional members of the House Judiciary Committee during the summer of 1998 as part of the campaign that led to the amendment of RECA in 2000.

The booklet has been requested by a number of teachers of grade school students. One of these teachers, from Crownpoint, New Mexico, had his eighth-grade Navajo students write essays after reading the booklet for class. An environmental program for schoolteachers distributed hundreds of copies to schools with significant numbers of Navajo students. Copies were also available for use at Diné College and the Crownpoint Institute of Technology. It is unlikely, given our liberal distribution method and lack of comprehensive tracking, that we will ever learn about most of the uses to which the booklet was put in classrooms.

At a conference about research and Navajo people in Shiprock, New Mexico, in January 1999, an evaluation of the booklet was conducted with the mostly Navajo (81.5 percent) audience. About one-half of those surveyed already knew about the booklet, and a majority had immediate family members who were uranium miners. Despite the large number of booklets that had been distributed in the Shiprock area, only 22.7 percent thought that many other Navajo people had seen it, or the exhibit, prior to the conference.

The results of the survey are presented in table 3. Respondents viewed the booklet positively (i.e., a low rank for "boring" and high ranks for "important" and other similarly positive terms). A few descriptors ranked toward the middle of the five-point scale, all of which related to emotional impact ("depressing," "upsetting"). Respondents were rarely moderate in their responses to these questions. For example, most ranked the book either very depressing and or not at all depressing. This could reflect a difference in interpretation of these questions. Clearly the subject matter was depressing, but it is possible that some respondents found the book uplifting in spite of this.

TABLE 3 **Survey results**

VARIABLE	AVERAGE RATING (1=not at all; 5=very)	VALID NUMBER
Boring	1.67	21
Irrelevant	2.53	19
Upsetting	3.00	19
Depressing	3.10	20
Too emotional	3.25	20
Accurate	4.10	20
Respects Navajo culture	4.16	19
Educational	4.24	21
Professional	4.35	20
Useful	4.45	20
Moving	4.45	20
Well done	4.55	20
Important	4.86	21

The Exhibit

Informal short-term shows of the exhibit were held in several communities prior to the funding of a full-scale tour (table 4). In addition, a second set of photographic images was produced for use in less-formal displays (i.e., those for which the expense of transporting the entire framed exhibit was excessive). Informal shows generally attracted audiences of between 20 and 100 people. The very first show, in Shiprock, also provided an opportunity for some of the persons interviewed to review their oral statements and to make minor changes and/or additions. A more unusual use of the informal display was at a talk by a Navajo uranium activist in Concord, Massachusetts.

TABLE 4 **Shows of the exhibit**

FULL EXHIBITIONS	INFORMAL/SHORT TERM
Diné College, Tsaile, AZ	Diné College, Shiprock, NM
Utah State University, Logan, UT	Navajo Tribal Council, Window Rock, AZ
Navajo Nation Museum, Window Rock, AZ	Navajo Studies Conference, Albuquerque, NM

FULL EXHIBITIONS	INFORMAL/SHORT TERM
Tufts University, Medford, MA	Crownpoint, NM (2x)
Seattle Central Community College, Seattle, WA	Concord, MA
University of New Mexico, Albuquerque, NM	ATSDR/CDC, Atlanta, GA
National Atomic Museum, Albuquerque, NM	
Misericordia College, Dallas, PA	
West Virginia University, Morgantown, WV	

A full-scale, subsidized tour (tables 4 and 5), coordinated by a professional exhibit-touring service, began in April 1998. Each of the shows during the tour had an opening program or reception, and in some cases additional programs were held. Our audiences could be divided into those who attended programs held in conjunction with each show of the exhibit, and those who viewed the exhibit independent of a program.

We held 18 public programs and presentations during the course of the funded tour, which ended in October 1999, with a total attendance of about 745 people, one-third of whom were Navajo people (table 5). In some cases, such as the show at the University of New Mexico, other tribes were among the viewers, including members of pueblos near Los Alamos National Laboratory. These program attendees received first-hand testimony by Navajo people affected by uranium mining, and background documentary information about the historical events that led to the uranium-mining tragedy. Subsequent to the funded tour, we contracted with a touring service, which promoted the exhibit and arranged three shows—one in Pennsylvania and one in West Virginia (both in coal-mining communities), and one in St. Louis, Missouri.

Excluding the show at the University of New Mexico, for which we do not have attendance estimates, there were about 4,370 viewers of the exhibit by 1999 (table 5). This is, by any standard, a sizable number of people, but underestimates the actual outreach for several reasons. First, dissemination of the

TABLE 5 **Exhibitions, dates, programs, attendance, and speakers through 1999.**

EXHIBITIONS	DATES	PROGRAMS	EXHIBIT ATTENDANCE (APPROX.)	PROGRAM ATTENDANCE (% NAVAJO)	SPEAKERS
Diné College	3/30/98–4/10/98	Opening program	120	50 (90%)	Benally, Tsosie
		Lectures in classes		70 (100%)	Brugge
Utah State University	4/16/98–5/29/98	Reception	500	100 (0%)	—
		Public talk		25 (0%)	Brugge, Tsosie
Navajo Nation Museum	6/8/98–8/14/98	Opening program	700	50 (95%)	Harrison, Benally, Navajo EPA, miners and widows
Tufts University	6/10/98–7/30/98	Opening program	2,000	45 (3%)	Benally, Tsosie
		College class		50 (0%)	Tsosie
		Medical School		12 (8%)	Benally, Tsosie
		Fletcher School		20 (0%)	Brugge
		Medical class		80 (0%)	Brugge
Seattle Community College	12/10/98–12/18/98	Day program	350	10 (0%)	Benally
		Night program		20 (0%)	Benally
University of New Mexico	1/23/99–4/31/99	Members reception	Pending	25 (0%)	—
		Opening program		40 (20%)	Brugge, Benally, Johnson, Frank
Subtotal			3,670	600 (29%)	
Other activities					
Los Alamos, NM		Training for tribes		20 (0%)	Benally
Richland, WA		Training for tribes		25 (0%)	Brugge
Myrtle Beach, SC		Nat. Congress, Am. Indians		?	Benally
Washington, DC		Lobby Congress		—	Tsosie
Shiprock, NM		Conference talk		100 (80%)	Brugge, Benally
Atlanta, GA		Informal exhibit	700		—
TOTAL			**4,370**	**745 (34%)**	

booklet proceeded apace with the exhibit and reached thousands more individuals—many of whom, we believe, have shown it to a circle of friends and colleagues. Second, press coverage informed, albeit in less detail, a still broader audience. Third, a number of Web sites that displayed part of the exhibit also had large numbers of visits. In fact, the Boston University Web site had 24,000 visitors in 1998 (for six exhibits, of which the Navajo uranium miners were one).

The project generated sporadic print, radio, and television coverage, including articles in *Peacework* (American Friends Service Committee), the *Navajo Times*, the *Gallup (NM) Independent*, *Tufts Medicine*, and *American Indian Review*. The *Tufts Medicine* article was the central feature of that issue, covering eight pages with photographs and quotes from the book. The issue also included a profile of Doug Brugge as a faculty member (Morgan 1998). A radio interview was aired by the radio station at Utah State University, and the public-access TV station from Farmington, New Mexico, covered the exhibit when it was at the Navajo Nation Museum in Window Rock, Arizona. Articles have also been sent to us from Japan and Siberia, where the project figured in stories about nuclear power and uranium mining respectively.

There was one request by a viewer to purchase a print of one of the photographs. This raised ethical issues for the project team because we had not asked the interviewees whether they consented to having their photographs displayed for personal use. This was resolved when Timothy Benally contacted the interviewee in question and obtained agreement to have the print sold. The fee charged was then transmitted to the individual in the photograph, minus printing costs.

Videotape

The videotape, called *Uranium: The Navajo Nuclear Legacy*, has been shown both as an accompaniment to the exhibit and as part of speaking engagements by members of the project team. Since it was never envisioned as a stand-alone or comprehensive documentary, this is its most appropriate use. Nevertheless, we have received requests for copies of the tape from museums, college professors, and community activists. The fact that we produced the videotape has opened the door to participating in other video documentary projects. Project staff and advisors have consulted with the producer of a PBS documentary of a Navajo family that includes their experiences with uranium mining (*The Return of Navajo Boy*, produced by Jeff Spitz and Bennie Klain, 2000).

Newsletter

Early in the project, we began publishing a newsletter on an ad hoc basis. Seven issues, ranging in size from four to ten pages, were published from winter 1996 to spring 2001. Original articles were written by members of the project team, by advisory-board members, and by professional journalists. In addition, articles from newspapers and other sources were occasionally reprinted (with permission). The newsletter grew to have an address list of over 700 people, and in addition to being a valuable and up-to-date educational tool, it has also generated donations for the project.

Archive

Two archives now exist for project materials. One is at the Center for Southwest Research at the University of New Mexico in Albuquerque. The other, more complete archive is retained by the Navajo Nation Museum in Window Rock, Arizona. At least one book has drawn on the interviews that we conducted, focusing on emotional expression as activism among Navajos (Schwarz 2001). The author thought that the deep public sharing of emotions by widows and daughters of miners recorded in our project were significant, given the cultural traditions of the Navajo people.

Role of Oral Evidence

It may be of interest to readers to consider how this project does or does not affect the legitimacy with which oral testimony by Native Americans is viewed. Because Native Americans have no written history preceding modern times, and because Native Americans also have strong oral traditions, their oral record is particularly important. The case of uranium mining and the Navajo people falls between the extremes of a strong written record and a completely oral record, illustrating how oral tradition can be relevant even in contemporary situations. There is documentation of many aspects of the Navajo experience with uranium mining, including books and scientific studies. These written records, however, are missing at least some of the points made by Navajo people that we interviewed. For example, the exposure of the wives of the miners to uranium-laced dust through the clothing that their husbands brought home has not been part of the scientific studies conducted to date.

Secondary Goals

We feel that our primary objective, education of Navajo people and non-Navajo audiences, has been largely successful and will likely continue with the publication of this volume. We also have seen some progress on secondary goals.

Although we are unaware of use of the booklet in Navajo-language classes, we have been able to generate scientific hypotheses, another of our secondary objectives. In recent years, increased attention has begun to be paid to the lifestyle-based differences in environmental risk that Native American populations face (e.g., Harris and Harper 1997). In this context, project members submitted comments to the U.S. EPA about their environmental assessment of the King Tutt Mines near Shiprock, raising concern that their evaluation may not adequately consider exposure pathways to the Navajo people living near these abandoned mining areas. In response to comments by project members, the Navajo EPA, and others, U.S. EPA proposed conducting a risk assessment based on Navajo lifestyles (Levon Benally, Navajo EPA, personal communication, March 1998; Teresa Coons, personal communication, August 2001).

We also evaluated the interviews for environmental, health, and safety issues raised by interviewees to elucidate aspects of the impact of uranium mining on the Navajo people that had not yet been evaluated. Qualitative review identified issues that probably deserve investigation (see table 6).

TABLE 6 **Possible route of exposure to the community**

PAST	PRESENT
Contamination brought home on miner's clothing	Playing around or in abandoned mines
Ate yellowcake (conc. uranium) as pollen substitute in ceremonies	Herding sheep around or in abandoned mines
Eating contaminated livestock or wildlife	Eating contaminated livestock or wildlife
Ambient environmental contamination	Ambient environmental contamination
Building homes with mine wastes	
Playing on mine/mill tailing piles	
Visiting fathers/husbands at the mine	
Living next to the active mines	
Drinking contaminated water	

A point raised by one of the children of a miner that we interviewed was the lack of mental-health counseling for the families of miners who are ill or deceased (see Kathlene Tsosie-Blackie in Brugge et al. 1997; see also chapter 7). In some communities, most of the men from older generations worked in mines, and many have died or are sick. The result has been that their families and friends are traumatized by loss of husbands, fathers, and grandfathers before their time. Despite this, there are few counseling services available.

Something that became apparent only after we had produced the book and exhibit was that the approach we employed was of interest to other environmentally affected communities as a model (e.g., Quigley 1997). Indeed, Brugge and Benally were part of a training team for members of Native American tribal governments in New Mexico and Washington State. The training was for a consortium of ten tribes and was designed to assist them with their project to document the Native American point of view, which was left out of the U.S. Department of Energy's

summary of environmental impacts of nuclear development
(USDOE 1996).

Brugge (1997a, 1997b) has written toxicological profiles of
uranium and radium under contract with the Nuclear Risk
Management for Native Communities (NRMNC) project. One
of these has been published in an academic journal (Brugge
et al. 2005). NRMNC is based at Clark University in
Massachusetts and works with Native communities in
Oklahoma, New Mexico, and Nevada. With NRMNC, we
(Brugge and Benally) also held a workshop with schoolteachers
at Laguna Pueblo in New Mexico (site of the massive "Jackpile"
open-pit uranium mine) with the idea that they could have
their students do an oral history and photography project. To
date, the effort to launch that oral-history project has been
held up because of lack of funding.

In addition, Brugge has reviewed the toxicological literature
relating to heavy-metal and radiological constituents of uranium ore (table 7). There were numerous associations with disease documented for contaminants in uranium ore. We believe
that further investigation of health risk to Navajo people who
live today or have lived in the past in close proximity to uranium-mining activities is warranted.

TABLE 5 **Uranium ore constituents and key diseases seen in
either human populations or experimental animals.
Those cancers in parentheses are scientifically
weaker associations.**

CONSTITUENTS	CANCERS	OTHER DISEASES
Uranium*	(Lung, bone, stomach, brain, and skin)	Kidney damage, birth defects, reduced sperm count, skin irritation, pulmonary fibrosis, liver damage, and nervous system harm.
Radium*	Bone, nasal sinuses and mastoid air cells, leukemia, (eye, breast, liver, kidney, and nervous system)	Bone and blood effects at very high levels, possibly cataracts.

CONSTITUENTS	CANCERS	OTHER DISEASES
Radon*	Lung	Pulmonary fibrosis at very high levels.
Thorium*	(Liver, bone, leukemia, pancreas, lymph, hematopoietic system, and lung)	Cirrhosis of the lungs, blood changes, and altered liver enzyme levels.
Low LET ionizing radiation (basically external dose)	Acute and chronic myelogenous leukemia, lung, stomach, breast, (thyroid, bladder, nervous system, skin, oesophagus, colon, liver, and bone)	Radiation poisoning at high levels.
Vanadium	None	Kidney, central nervous system effects (poss. including manic-depression), birth defects, and inhibition of key cellular enzymes. Cardiac palpitation, and lung, skin, and eye irritation. May be an essential nutrient at low levels. Investigated as a treatment for diabetes because it is an insulin mimic.
Arsenic	Lung, skin, liver, bladder, and (kidney)	Causes hyper- and hypopigmentation and hyperkeratosis of the skin. Toxic to the nervous system, can cause jaundice (liver), and can alter heart functioning. Causes peripheral vascular disease, blood changes, chromosomal aberrations and may lead to birth defects.
Magnesium	None	Neuropsychiatric disorder (similar to Parkinson's disease), liver and lung damage. Decreased male fertility.
Beryllium	Lung	Lung disease (berylliosis), skin hypersensitivity, immunological changes, kidney damage.

(* Radioactive element)

The general utility of the booklet, exhibit, and video, and the positive reactions that we observe lead us to believe that there is something generalizable in the nature and form of the project. One of the advantages of our approach is that it serves as a complement to the technical reports and statistics that tend to dominate environmental issues. Communities want something that is more fully their own and that expresses what they think and feel.

After all, oral history and photography are proud traditions in the development of social and economic justice. Seminal figures such as Studs Terkel and Dorothea Lange pioneered these approaches during the Great Depression. It is only natural that environmental justice for Native Americans would also be amenable to a variation on these time-tested and honored methods.

References

Austin-Garrison, M. B., B. Casaus, D. McLaughlin, C. Slate. 1996. *Dine' Bizaad Yissohigii*: The past present, and future of Navajo literacy. In E. Jelinek, S. Midgette, K. Rice, and L. Saxon, eds., *Athabaskan language studies: Essays in honor of Robert W. Young*, 349–89. Albuquerque: University of New Mexico Press.

Brugge, D. M. 1997. *Radium: Exposure pathways and health effects: Nuclear risk management for native communities*. Worcester, MA: G. P. Marsh Institute, Clark University.

Brugge, D. M., T. H. Benally. 1998. Navajo Indian voices and faces testify to the legacy of uranium mining. *Cultural Survival Quarterly* 22:16–19.

Brugge, D. M., T. Benally, P. Harrison, M. Austin-Garrison, L. Fasthorse-Begay. 1997. *Memories come to us in the rain and the wind: Oral histories and photographs of Navajo uranium miners and their families*. Boston: Tufts School of Medicine.

Brugge, D., T. Benally, P. Harrison, M. Austin-Garrison, C. Stilwell, M. Elsner, K. Bomboy, H. Johnson, L. Fasthorse-Begay. 1999. The Navajo Uranium Miner Oral History and Photography Project. In J. Piper, ed., *Dine Baa Hane Bi Naaltsoos: Collected papers from the seventh through the tenth Navajo Studies Conferences*, 85–96. Window Rock, AZ: Navajo Nation Historic Preservation Department.

Brugge, D., J. L. deLemos, B. Oldmixon. 2005. A review of exposure pathways and health effects associated with chemical and radiological toxicity of natural uranium. *Reviews on Environmental Health* 20, no. 3 (2005): 177–94.

Brugge, D., P. Hynes. 2005. Introduction: Science with the people. In D. Brugge, P. Hynes, eds., *Community research in environmental health: Studies in science, advocacy and ethics*. Aldershot, England: Ashgate Publishing Ltd.

Crank, D. L. 1997. Uranium miners, relatives recall yellow-water days, *Gallup (NM) Independent*, November 13, 8.

Dawson, S. E., P. H. Perry, P. Harrison Jr. 1997. Advocacy and social action among Navajo uranium workers and their families. In *Social work in health settings: Practice in context*, 2nd ed., 391–407. New York and London: Haworth Press.

Eichstaedt, P. H. 1994. *If you poison us: Uranium and Native Americans*. Santa Fe, NM: Red Crane Books.

Harris, S. G., B. L. Harper, 1997. A Native American exposure scenario. *Risk Analysis* 17 (6): 789–95.

Kelley, M. 1997. Miners casualties of cold war. *Albuquerque Journal* [n.d.], A4.

Morgan, B. 1998. Adrift in the rain and the wind. *Tufts Medicine* 58, no. 1: inside cover and 28–35.

Quigley, D. 1997. Book review. In *The Childhood Cancer Research Institute Newsletter* (Worcester, MA: G. P. Marsh Institute, Clark University), 14.

Schwarz, M. T. 2001. *Navajo lifeways: Contemporary issues, ancient knowledge*. Norman, OK: University of Oklahoma Press.

Smith, M. 1997. Book review. In *The Workbook* (Albuquerque: Southwest Research and Information Center) 22, no. 3: 124–25.

Thompson, P. 1988. *The voice of the past: Oral history*. 2nd ed. Oxford and New York: Oxford University Press.

U.S. Department of Energy (USDOE), Office of Environmental Management. 1996. *Closing the circle on the splitting of the atom: The environmental legacy of the nuclear weapons production in the United States and what the Department of Energy is doing about it.* Washington, DC. U.S. DOE.

Index

Page numbers in bold type indicate photographs.

acculturation, 102, 106
activists, 75, 76, 185; comparison to activists of civil-rights period, 70; goals for, 67–68; and meeting places, 70; working with, 71
Advisory Committee on Human Radiation Experiments, 39
advocacy, 72
Akwesasne Mohawk Indians, 109
Alamogordo, NM, 2
Albuquerque, NM, 60, 161, 167, 183
Albuquerque Tribune, 38
alcohol abuse, 92, 101
A Little Water (Lapahie birthplace), 79
Aloysious, Anna, 95
Ambrosia Lake, NM, 126
American Indian Review, 190
American Psychiatric Association, 108
anxiety, 92, 96, 100–101
Archer, Victor, 32, 139, 140
Arizona, xv, 1, 4, 27, 59
arsenic, 195
Arthur, George, 173

atomic energy, 1
Atomic Energy Act, 174
Atomic Energy Commission (AEC), 27, 119, 123; as obstacle, 33; and PHS, 34
attorney fees, 19, 66
Austin-Garrison, Martha, 182
Australian aboriginals, 185

Bale, William, 31
Beaverlodge, Saskatchewan, 40
Begay, Kee, 14
Begay, Paul, 120
Begay, Raymond, 120
Begay v. United States, 42, 63
BEIR IV, 140, 141, 142–43
Benally, Dan N., 95–96
Benally, Timothy, xv, xvii, 66, 117, 129, 181, 182, 190, 193; interview with George Tutt, 11–23; interview with Mary Louise Johnson and Minnie Tsosie, 155–65
Bennie Martinez Mining Company, 130
Bergkrankheit, 26
Berwell Mining Company, 50
beryllium, 33, 195
Billy, Ervin, 63

Biological Effects of Ionizing
    Radiation (BEIR), 40
Bitl'aabito', 49
black lung disease, 33
Bomboy, Katherine, 183
Brugge, Doug, xv, 97, 181, 182,
    190, 193, 194
Buffalo Creek dam disaster, 92
Bureau of Indian Affairs (BIA),
    xvi; and discovery of ura-
    nium on Navajo Nation
    lands, 2; Indian Service
    Population, 102; and
    Treaty of 1868, 30

California, xvi
cancer, 158
Canyon City, CO, 130
Capitan, Rita and Mitchell,
    168; interview with,
    167–75
Carrizo Mountains, 27
Catholic Church, 169
C. B. Johnson Mining
    Company, 130
Changing Woman, 6
chapter meetings, 70
Charley, Harris, 40, 58
Charley, Perry, 40, 42, 57, 61,
    64, 65, 69, 71, 73–75;
    development of video in
    Navajo language, 68
Chemawa, OR, 79
Chernobyl nuclear disaster, 99
children, 4, 51–52, 71, 92, 96,
    98, 99, 102, 132–33, 158,
    160–64; exposure to radi-
    ation, 18, 20; and safe
    water, 172
Choney, S. K., 102
Christian faith healing, 109
Churchill, W., 103
Church Rock, NM, 27, 96, 146,
    167; dam break at, 4, 96,

104; proposed mine
    at, 173
Church Rock Uranium
    Workers, 146
Clark, R., 103
Clark University, 194
clothing, 51, 52
coal miners: uprising of, 37
Cold War, xvi, 3
Colorado, 1, 11, 12, 13, 15, 27, 39,
    55, 58, 59, 121
Colorado Plateau Uranium
    Workers, 146
Colorado Uranium Workers
    Council, 146
Community Health
    Representative (CHR)
    Program, 62
Concord, MA, 187
Congressional hearings, 39, 70
contamination, 91, 94–97,
    104; and routes of expo-
    sure, 193
Cooper, T. W., 107, 108
cor pulmonale, 139
Cortez, CO, 130
Cove, AZ, xvi, 27, 42, 62, 86, 94,
    121, 129, 133, 155, 161, 181;
    Navajo Uranium Mine
    near, **18**, **29**; widows of
    miners in, 37
Crank, Dan, 184
crime, alcohol-related, 5
Crownpoint Chapter
    House, 172
Crownpoint Institute of
    Technology, 186
Crownpoint, NM, 86, 146, 167,
    174, 184, 186; proposed
    mine at, 173
Crownpoint Uranium
    Project, 173
Csordas, T. J., 108
Curie, Marie and Pierre, 2

Czechoslovakia, 26–27, 30

dams, 4, 92
Daniel, Pat, 16
Dawson, Susan E., 57, 60, 65,
    72, 74, 97, 101
Denver, CO, 60
Department of Energy, 38, 68,
    104, 141, 185, 193
Department of Interior: Office
    of Surface Mining
    Control Reclamation and
    Enforcement, 68
Department of Justice (DOJ),
    59, 137–39, 141, 185, 186
depression, 92, 96, 100–101
Deswood, Peter, 125
diabetes, 158
Diné, 1
Diné CARE, 146
Diné College, 99, 104, 181,
    183, 186
disasters: adverse psychologi-
    cal outcomes of, 92; con-
    ceptualizations of, 91–93;
    environmental, 103; and
    psychological scars of
    trauma, 91–92
discrimination, 102
diseases, 194–95. *See also spe-
    cific diseases*
Donald L. mine, 17
Dove Creek, CO, 119, 130
Durango, CO, 158

Eastern Navajo Agency, 173
Eastern Navajo Diné Against
    Uranium Mining
    (ENDAUM), 171, 172, 173
Eastern Navajo Uranium
    Workers, 146
education: and emotional
    recovery and healing, 105
Education Foundation of

America, 181
Egnar, CO, 130
Eichstaedt, Peter, 37
Ellison, Jimmy, 125
Elsner, Mary, 183
emphysema, 33
employment, 91, 124; close to
    home, 15
Energy Employees
    Occupational Illness
    Compensation Program
    Act (EEOICPA),
    145–47, 151
environment: sacred nature
    of, 106
environmental contamination,
    91; and technological dis-
    aster, 75
environmental devastation, 95
environmental losses, 94–97
Environmental Protection
    Agency, 104, 134, 135, 181,
    185, 192
environmental racism, 90,
    103, 172
exposure records: inaccuracy
    of, 143–44
Exxon Valdez oil spill, 96

Farmington, NM, 190
Fasthorse-Begay, Lydia, 182
Federal Tort Claims Act
    (FTCA), 58
Fermi, Enrico, 2
First Nations of Australia, 9
Five Mountains, 14
Floyd, Frank, 97
Fogarty, John, 167
Ford Foundation, 181
Fort Sumner, NM, 160
Four Corners area, xvi, 1, 5, 181
Four Corners Uranium Millers
    Association, 65
Frank, Mary, **90**, 97

Gad Ii'ahi, 49
Gaia, 8–9
Gallup Independent, 190
Gallup, NM, 4
George Energy Resource, 130
George, Jack, 14
George, Junior, 14
Germany, 26–27
ghost sickness syndrome, 108
Gillette Syndrome, 5
Gilliland, Frank, 42
Gold Room, 128
Gottlieb, Leon S., 60
Grand Junction, CO, 119
Grants, NM, 39
grazing, 4, 5
Green, B. L., 92
group action: as weapon, 8

hantavirus, 4
Harley, John, 31
harmony: restoration of, 108
Harrison, Phil, 42, 57, **61**, 61,
    65, 66, 67, 68, 74, 181;
    elected chairman of Red
    Valley Committee, 64;
    and international travel,
    70; interview with Joe
    Ray Harvey, 129–35;
    interview with Leroy and
    Lorraine Jack, 49–56;
    interview with Tommy
    James, 117–28
Harrison, Phillip, Sr., 58
Harvey, Joe Ray, 94, **130**; inter-
    viewed by Harrison,
    129–35
Harvey, Sam, 13
Haskie, Leonard, 63
Hatch amendments, 150–51
Hatch, Orrin, 40, 58
Hattis, D., 141
Hawks Nest, WV, 33
healing: culturally specific

forms of, 106–9;
    resources for, 109; spiri-
    tual, 108; and traditional
    beliefs, 108
healing ceremonies, 109
Hero Twins, 6
Hibakusha, 61–62
high blood pressure, 158
Hiroshima, Japan, 61
Holaday, Duncan, 33, 34,
    142, 144
*Homeland: Four Portraits of
    Native Action* (film), 167
Home State Company, 130
Honig, R. G., 92
Hopi Indians, 6
Hosh, 79
House, Benjamin, 170
houses: contaminated, 4, 161;
    death in, 72; use of
    radioactive stones and
    protore in building, 96
hózho, 108–9
Hueper, Wilhelm, 31; speaking
    and travel restrictions
    on, 34
human loss and bereavement,
    93–94
Hydro Resources, Inc., 168,
    173, 174

Indian Health Service, 62, 73,
    181; hospitals of, 59
Indian reservations: resource
    extraction from, 103
Indians: and health care, 4. *See
    also* Indian Health
    Service (IHS)
Inuit Indians, 110

Jachimov, Czechoslovakia, 26
Jack, Leroy and Lorraine, **50**;
    interviewed by Harrison,
    49–56

Jackpile open-pit mine,
    145, 194
James, Tommy, **118**; inter-
    viewed by Harrison,
    117–28
Japan, 70, 190
Jerusalem, M., 97, 104
Jicarilla Apache Reservation, 4
Joachimsthal,
    Czechoslovakia, 30
Johnson, Helen, 97–98, 181
Johnson, Mary Louise, **156**;
    interviewed by Benally,
    155–65
Jones, Sam, 40

Kayenta, AZ, 27, 184
Kennedy, John F., 38
Kennedy, Ted, 58
Kerr McGee, 119, 122, 125, 129,
    130, 131
Kiiyaa'aanii, 79
Kingsville Dome mine, 175
King Tutt Mines, 192
Kirtland, NM, 128

LaDuke, W., 103
Laguna Pueblo, 145, 194
Lange, Dorothea, 196
Lapahie, Daisy, 79
Lapahie, George, **80**, 99; inter-
    viewed by Benally, 79–87
La Sal Mountain, 12, 14, 83
leachate mining, 124, 168, 170,
    171, 173, 184
Leetso, 9, 14, 105; birth of, 2–3;
    slaying of, 5–8; victims
    of, 3
leukemia, 141
Long Park, 16
Lorenz, Egon, 31
Lovelace Research Center, 99
Lukachukai Uranium
    Workers, 146

lung cancer, xvii, 32, 59, 73, 93,
    100, 138, 139, 141; causal
    agent identified for ura-
    nium miners, 30–31;
    mortality rates, 41; and
    radon exposure, 41, 144;
    and smoking, 36, 41; and
    uranium mining, 35,
    60, 61

Madsen, Gary E., 57, 60, 101
magnesium, 195
Manhattan Project, 2
Manson, S. M., 102
Massachusetts, 194
Mazzocchi, Anthony, 37, 38
McCabe, Edward, 125
McFarlane, A. C., 106
Mesa Verde, CO, 157
Metal Engineering, 119
mill sites: abandoned, 104
mill workers, 58; registry
    for, 62
Miners' Colfax Medical
    Center, 62
Mitten Rock, NM, 14
Mobil Oil, 169
monster: naming of, 2
Monument Valley, UT, 27, 125
Morgan, Frank, 105
Mother Earth, 6
Mount Taylor, NM, 3, 6, 39
Mt. La Sal, UT, 81
Mt. Rose, NM, 161
Mutton Man, 4

Nagasaki, Japan, 62
Nakaidenae, Paul, 98
National Academy of
    Sciences, 40
National Cancer Institute, 34
National Environmental
    Justice Advisory
    Council, 185

National Institute of
Environmental Health
Sciences, 104
National Institute of
Occupational Safety and
Health (NIOSH), 38; pro-
posed worker-protection
revisions never imple-
mented, 42
national security issue, 39
Native American Church, 109
Native Americans: and smok-
ing, 36; as victims of
nuclear technology, 179
Naturita, CO, 13, 14, 16, 21,
79, 80
Navajo Abandoned Mine
Lands Reclamation
(AML) Department,
68, 104
Navajo Community
College, 181
Navajo Environmental
Protection Agency,
104, 192
Navajo Environmental
Protection Commission,
64
Navajo lands, xv; abandoned
uranium mine shafts on,
28; and uranium ore, 3
Navajo language, 1, 3, 30, 68,
104, 107, 179–80, 182, 192
Navajo Nation, xv, 1, 27; abandoned mines in, 3;
dependency upon BIA,
xvi; IHS hospitals on, 59;
map of, 28; and Office of
the Navajo Uranium
Workers (ONUW), xvii;
and problems with gov-
ernment-provided health
care, 30; schools and colleges in, 184; and stock

reduction, xvi; unwillingness of officials to finan-
cially support
replacement of contami-
nated homes, 64; and
wage economy, 5, 28
Navajo Nation Council, 172
Navajo Nation Historic
Preservation
Department, 181
Navajo Nation Museum, 190
Navajo people, xv–xviii, 1–8, 12,
14, 17, 29, 30, 52, 56, 85,
188; advocacy and social
action, 57–76; and com-
munication ethics, 107;
contaminated by mine
water, 134; cultural practices of, 95; and extended
family networks, 71; feelings of betrayal, 97–98;
organizing of, 42; psy-
chological effects of
environmental disasters
on, 85–110; psychological
well-being and environ-
mental stability, 107; and
smoking, 36–41; spiritual
ties to land, 95; and
taboo about death, 107
Navajo RECA Reform Working
Group, 146
Navajo Reservation, 27, 35, 62,
167; no unionization of
miners, 38
Navajo Studies
Conference, 183
Navajo Times, 190
Navajo Tribal Council, 2, 38
Navajo Tribe, xv, 62, 134; and
BIA, 30; no word in lan-
guage for radiation, 30
Navajo Uranium Mine, **18**,
29, 134

Navajo Uranium Miner Oral
History and Photography
Project, xv, xviii, 177–96;
archives of, 191; booklet
for, 183–87; and educa-
tion, 179; exhibit for, 182,
187–90; funding for, 181,
182; goal of, 177; methodology of, 180–83;
newsletter for, 191; survey
of response to booklet,
186–87; touring of exhib-
it, 188–90; video for, 182,
190–91
Navajo widows, xvii–xviii, 71,
133, 155–65; interviews
with, 72–73; organizing
of, 36–37
Nebraska, 13
Nevada, 4, 82, 194
Nevada Test Site, 138
Newfoundland, 40
New Mexico, xv, 1, 4, 27, 59, 173,
175, 193, 194; and closure
of uranium mines in
exceedance of 10 WL
limit, 35; guidelines for
radon exposure, 34
noise, 51, 83
Northern Navajo Medical
Center, 62
Nucla, CO, 16
nuclear accidents: Chernobyl
accident, 99; largest in
U.S., 96; Three Mile
Island incident, 96
nuclear bombs: first explosion
of, 2; testing of, 4, 39, 138
nuclear power: and abuse,
9–10
Nuclear Regulatory
Commission (NRC),
167–68, 174; Atomic
Safety and Licensing
Board of, 173
Nuclear Risk Management for
Native Communities, 194
nuclear waste, 21; storage of, 3
Nuremberg Code, 32

Oak Springs, AZ, 11, 64, 120
Office of Navajo Uranium
Workers, 59, 62, 63, 65,
66, 69, 84, 181; registering
with, 67
Ogdan, UT, 130
Oil, Chemical, and Atomic
Workers International, 37
Oklahoma, 194
Ontario, 40
oral history, 177–78, 191–92
Owens, Wayne, 58

Peacework, 190
Pelizza, Mark, 170
Pennsylvania, 188
Pete, John, 14
peyote, 109
Phoenix, AZ, xvi
pneumoconiosis, 59, 93, 139
pneumonia, 33
Portland, OR, 83
posttraumatic stress disorder,
92, 96; and threat to personal integrity, 102
poverty, 101–3
President's Advisory
Committee on
Human Radiation
Experimentation, 70
protore, 95, 96
Public Health Service (PHS),
xvii, 83, 142; and AEC, 34;
study by, 32, 35
pulmonary fibrosis, 139

racism, 90, 101–3, 172; reactions to, 103

radiation: education about, 62;
no Navajo word for, 30
radiation exposure, 99, 133,
139; education about, 67;
studies on effects of, 62
Radiation Exposure
Compensation Act of
1990 (RECA), xviii, 18, 19,
25, 37, 54, 58, 63, 65,
75–76, 137–53; and all or
nothing compensation,
140; amendments adopt-
ed in 2000, 146, 150–51,
186; applying for com-
pensation under, 67;
budget for, 147; burden of
1990 application process,
148; compensable med-
ical conditions under,
139; compensation
awarded due to, 42;
compensation benefits
delayed, 43; and com-
pensation claims, 138;
compensation program
framed in form of apolo-
gy, 138; compensation
schedule, 58–59; and
denial of claims, 85,
141; difficulties encoun-
tered in efforts to comply
with, 73, 100; and expo-
sure data, 138–39; and
failure to compensate
deserving claims, 141;
inadequacy of compen-
sation, 123, 163; meetings
about, 68; proposed
changes to, 149–50;
purpose of, 138; reform
of compensation
process, 185–86; and
restrictive regulations,
132; scope of coverage,

138; stringent conditions
for compensation,
141, 144
radioactive colonialism, 103
radioactive dust, 4
radioactive tailings, 64
radioactive waste, 4, 95, 104,
127–28
radioactive water, 96
radiological effects: no word
in Navajo vocabulary
for, 104
radium, 27, 194
radon, 30–31, 38, 138, 139, 140,
142, 195; dose/response
relationship, 40; expo-
sure to, and smoking, 40;
lung cancer and, 144;
measuring, 33, 35; and
ventilation, 34
radon daughters, 31
railroads, xvi, xvii, 13, 15, 82
Rainbow Serpent, 9
Redhouse, Leo, 40
Red Mesa, AZ, 121
Red Mesa/Mexican Water Four
Corners Uranium
Committee, 42, 65
Red Rock Chapter, xvii
Red Valley, AZ, 37, 42, 62, 63,
155, 181
Red Valley Committee, 64
Reistrup, J. V., 37
relationship problems: disasters and, 92
respect: as weapon, 8
respiratory disease, nonmalignant, 26, 33, 60–61,
138, 142
respiratory problems, 16
The Return of Navajo Boy, 191
Rio Puerco, 4, 96
Round Rock, AZ, 117
Ruth Mott Fund, 181

Saccomanno Research
Institute, 99
Safe Drinking Water Act, 174
safety, 80–81, 121, 131
safety equipment, 51
Salt Canyon, AZ, 12
Salt Lake City, UT, 40
Salzburg, Austria, 9, 70
Samet, Jonathan, 32
San Juan River, 134
Schneeberg, Germany, 26
schools, 63, 119, 120, 124, 167,
179, 183, 184, 186; contam-
inated, 4
"Seeing with a Native Eye:
How Many Sheep Will It
Hold?" (Tolkein), 6
Senate Committee on Labor
and Public Welfare, 37
Shamway Dayton Mining
Company, 130
sheep, 13, 69, 97; drinking con-
taminated water, 134
Shields, Lora, 20, 63, 68, 74
Shiprock High School, 120
Shiprock Hospital, 73
Shiprock Navajo Community
College, 63
Shiprock, NM, xvii, 5, 11, 27, 49,
65, 68, 84, 86, 99, 120, 125,
134, 183, 184, 187, 192
Shirley, Joe, Jr., 172
Shuey, Chris, 167
Siberia, 190
Sidney and Delaney, 119
silica dust, 142
silicosis, 33, 59, 139, 142
Slick Rock, CO, 55, 130
smoking, 139–41; ceremonial,
36; as complicating risk
factor in study of health
effects of uranium min-
ing, 36, 40; and defining
a smoker, 140; as a modi-
fier of risk, 142; and
Native Americans, 143
social action, 71, 72
somatic complaints, 92
Southwest Research and
Information Center
(SRIC), 167, 173
spiritual healing, 108
Stilwell, Chenoa Bah, 181, 183
St. Louis, MO, 188
stress, 100, 103–4
Sturgeon, D., 91
Surgeon General's 1964 report
on smoking and
health, 36
sweat lodge, 109
Sweetwater, AZ, 73

tailings, 4
Taneezahnii, 79
technological/human-caused
disasters, 90
Terkel, Studs, 196
Thompson, P., 178
thorium, 96, 195
Tlo'aashchioii, 79
Toadlena, NM, 84
tobacco: ceremonial use of, 36
Tódichiinii, 79
Tolkein, Barry, 6–8
Tome, Harry, 37, 38, 39, 40
Tonalea, AZ, 65
Tósidoh, 79
toxic waste, 3, 4, 103
trauma, 102
traumatic bereavement, 94
Treaty of 1868, xvi, 30
Tsé Alnaazti, 79
Tsé Dijol, 13
Tso, Harold, 40
Tsoodzil (sacred mountain), 3
Tsosie-Blackie, Kathlene, 106,
184, 186
Tsosie, Lewis, 158

Tsosie, Minnie, 99, **157**; inter-
    viewed by Benally, 155–65
Tsosie, Robertson, 158
tuberculosis, 33
Tufts Medicine, 190
Tufts University School of
    Medicine, 180
Tuskegee Study, 32
Tutt, George, **12**; interviewed
    by Benally, 11–23
Two Grey Hills, 79

Udall, Stewart, 38, 39, 42,
    63, 74
Udall, Tom, 173
Union Carbide, 17, 81, 130
United Nuclear
    Corporation, 96
University of New Mexico, 74,
    181, 188
University of New Mexico
    Cancer Research
    Center, 99
University of New Mexico
    School of Medicine, 62
uranium, 13, 14, 22, 55, 79–80,
    194; and corn pollen, 105,
    172; Diné conception of,
    105–6; exposure to, 54;
    milling of, 57; as mon-
    ster, 2; no word in Navajo
    vocabulary for, 104; and
    tumors, 86, 99; U.S. gov-
    ernment demand for, xvi
uranium disaster: comparison
    to Chernobyl disaster, 99;
    devastating psychologi-
    cal and social effects of,
    75; and long duration of
    psychological effects, 93;
    psychological effects of,
    93, 100–101; and psycho-
    logical intervention, 103;
    and suffering, 106

Uranium Education
    Center, 183
Uranium Education Program:
    development of glossary,
    104; efforts of, 104
uranium millers, 76; exclusion
    of, 145
uranium mills and milling, xv,
    75, 95
Uranium Mill Tailings
    Remediation and
    Control Act (UMTRCA)
    Project, 68
uranium miners, 17, 58, 76;
    attempt to get benefits
    for, 38; and CBS televi-
    sion network, 64; com-
    pensation received, 66;
    deaths of, xviii; and
    deliberate avoidance of
    health disaster by federal
    government, 42; dump-
    ing low-grade ore, **29**;
    and exclusion of minori-
    ty miners from PHS
    study, 35; illnesses
    among, 58; and labor
    unions, 37; and lack of
    documentation, 66; and
    lack of mental-health
    counseling, 193; and lung
    cancer, 41, 61; mistreat-
    ment of, 25; mortality
    risk of, 93; psychosocial
    effects of not being com-
    pensated for occupation-
    al illnesses, 57; registry
    for, 62; and smoking, 36;
    and use of outside
    resources, 74; violation
    of rights of, 42; wives
    of, 74
uranium mines, xvi, 3; aban-
    doned, xv, 68, 69, 86, 95,

104, 145; Donald L., 17;
and employment, xvii,
28; government inspec-
tion of, 35; homes next
to, 56; largest under-
ground, 6; map of, 28;
Navajo Uranium Mine,
18, 29, 134; and Navajo
workers, 3; proposed,
168; remediation of
abandoned mines, 68;
threat posed by aban-
doned, 69; and toxic
waste, 4; Vanadium
King, 17
uranium mining, 11; ban on,
172; beryllium and,
33–34; as compensable
occupational disease, 27;
dangers associated with,
xvii; as disruption of
Earth/Sky balance, 105–6;
efforts to resume, 100;
federal regulations for,
37–38; high degree of
community awareness
concerning the impact
of, 104; history of, 25–43;
and lung cancer, 30–31,
35, 41; Navajo cultural
interpretation of, 1; next
to schools and churches,
167; response to hazards
of, 33–34; and tailing
piles, 86
uranium ore, 3
Uranium Radiation Victims
Committee (URVC), 42,
63, 181
Uranium Resources, Inc., 170,
171, 174
*Uranium: The Navajo Nuclear
Legacy* (video documen-
tary), 190–91

uranium waste, 86; testing
of, 174
uranium workers: and health
problems, 85
Uravan, CO, 16, 120
U.S. Army Corps of
Engineers, 104
U.S. Geological Survey, 104
Utah, xv, 1, 12, 15, 27, 42, 59, 83
Utah Navajo
Downwinders, 146
Utah State University, 57, 190

vanadium, 13, 27, 195
Vanadium Corporation of
America, 12, 13, 27, 81
Vanadium King mine, 17
ventilation, 33–34, 51, 81, 121,
142; federal regulations
for, 42; lack of, 50, 53,
131; mechanical vs.
natural, 34
violence, 3; and alcohol, 5;
domestic, 5

war industry, 5, 8
Washburn Mining
Company, 131
Washington, 193
Washington Post, 37
water, 53, 80, 82, 119, 169; con-
taminated, 123, 133, 134,
159; EPA survey of quality
of, 96; and Safe Drinking
Water Act, 174; safety of,
172; testing of, 135
Waters, Frank, 6
Western Navajo Agency
Millers, 65
Western States RECA Reform
Coalition, 146; proposed
legislative changes to
RECA, 149–50
West Virginia, 92, 188

widows. *See* Navajo widows
Window Rock, AZ, 190
Witherspoon, G., 108
women, 3, 5, 192; and anxiety and depression, 92; exposure to radiation, 20; hardships experienced by wives of sick miners, 74; international network of, 9; and suffering, 134
Woody, R. L., 96–97, 101
workers' compensation, 39, 142
Working Level Months (WLM), 59, 139
Working Level (WL), 34; as

measurement for radon, 31–32
World Commission on the Environment, 8
World Uranium Hearing, 9, 70
Wyoming, 59

Yazzie-Lewis, Esther, xv, 1, 11, 49, 79, 117, 129, 155, 182
Yazzie, Rena, 159
Yeetso, 6
Yellow Bird mine, 12
yellowcake, 57

Zah, Petersen, 66
Zion, James and Elsie, 5